LIVE BETTER SOUTH OF THE BORDER IN

MEXICO

LIVE BETTER SOUTH OF THE BORDER IN

MEXICO

Practical Advice for Living and Working

THIRD EDITION

"Mexico" Mike™ Nelson

FULCRUM PUBLISHING
GOLDEN, COLORADO

Originally published by Roads Scholar Press, Mission, Texas, USA.
First Fulcrum trade paperback edition published April 2000.

Library of Congress Catalog Card No. 00132291

Printed in Canada
0 9 8 7 6 5 4 3 2 1

Editorial: Daniel Forrest-Bank
Design: Bill Spahr
Cover illustration: Mathew McFarren

Fulcrum Publishing
16100 Table Mountain Parkway, Suite 300
Golden, Colorado 80403
(800) 992-2908 • (303) 277-1623
www.fulcrum-books.com

Contents

vi

The Heartland—Colonial Mexico   *64*

The South   *83*

The Yucatán   *88*

The Pacific Coast   *93*

Introduction

This book is for people of all ages who want to live in Mexico and Central America, from retirees and baby boomers who want a new life to artists and writers who want a stimulating and less expensive way of life.

Mexico has a lot to offer someone who is thinking about living there. This book is for anyone of any age, from any country, who for any reason is thinking of living in Mexico for a few months or for many years. You could be one of the thousands of good people whose job has been eliminated by your corporation in the current "downsizing" of America. Your company may be sending you to Mexico to work for one of their branches. You might be an author or painter (or would like to become one) who wants to take some time to explore your creative self and create a masterpiece.

As a general rule, you can live on about two-thirds of what you live on at home. Most foreigners have incomes of $800–$1,200 a month. You can live on less if you are willing to be very frugal or choose a small town. No matter what you spend, your quality of life will be better.

You could be (like I was when I first moved to Mexico) simply at the end of your rope and need a safe place to get your head back together. You could be a woman or man who has just gotten out of a bad marriage and wants a place to figure out what life means or an entrepreneur planning on running a business.

You could be someone who is fed up with life on the treadmill in the USA who needs to take an unspecified amount of time off to find yourself again. And, of course, you could be a retiree (of any age) who is ready to try a different clime, now that you are out of the grind. I have met enough "retirees" in their forties and fifties to realize that **this large segment of**

people who move to Latin America are being ignored by "retirement" books. This book is also for people who are ready to retire in the traditional sense, who are in their sixties and seventies. Although many Canadians and Europeans live there as well as Americans, I have given prices in U.S. dollars. For Europeans, the exchange rate makes Latin America a very cheap place to live. For Canadians, it can still be a bargain.

I have included a brief overview of some Central American countries for those who want to get a general idea of what they are like compared to Mexico. In future editions, I will add more chapters about those countries. Meanwhile, this will give you the general idea. Most everything I say about culture and attitude is as applicable to Central America as it is to Mexico.

For many, retirement conjures up images of a lazy time in their lives, when they will sit back and take a long-deserved rest. Although living in Latin America is certainly less hectic than living in our urban or even rural society, it will require some effort to adapt to a different lifestyle and way of doing things. Retiring to Latin America means choosing how you want to spend your time. One thing that people living abroad have consistently asked me is to dispel the myth that they are merely living out their lives and doing nothing. These are the most active people I have ever known. Although some do flee south, buy or rent a little house and spend the rest of their lives watching sunsets, they are the exception. There are so many social activities and civic projects for retirees to be involved in that they must learn to manage their time or they will find themselves "working" too hard.

For those who are younger, there is an attraction to living abroad that is hard to deny. I did it in my twenties and thirties and found it to be a life-changing experience. I want this book to give you an idea of what your options are—not just in terms of different places to live, but in lifestyles to choose from. Above all, I would like to give you information about **how not to be an Ugly American.**

For some, moving to **"an American colony"** is exactly what they are after. This name is something of a misnomer. It does not mean that groups of Americans (and Canadians) are the only inhabitants of a town. It merely means that a large number of foreigners live in a community. They generally live in close proximity to each other in exclusive subdivisions, but there are usually several members of the foreign community who live in less expensive housing among the Mexican residents of the town. That is great if that is where you are at, and you will certainly find your place in the sun in Latin

America. For others, moving to a foreign culture means becoming immersed in it. I will give you tips on how to do that. Most people are somewhere in between. They want to experience and learn about the foreign culture, but they also want to be able to keep in touch with other foreigners. I will show you how to do that as well.

Let me introduce you to the joys (and drawbacks) of living in Mexico. **My purpose is not to encourage you to move there.** I want to give you an honest evaluation (subject to my prejudices) of what living in Mexico is like. It may or it may not be for you.

By the way, the average potential expatriate (a word that has nothing to do with one's patriotism, only with one's location) buys an average of three books on each country he or she is considering moving to. I recommend that you do the same. I have intentionally tried not to cover the same ground as most other "retirement" guides. Complex subjects like immigration laws, and laws about buying property and working, are best obtained from experts in those fields. I can consult with you personally about starting a business or living, for a reasonable fee. I will give you general information and suggest books from my bibliography. Although I have given some broad ranges of the cost of living, like housing, things change. The peso is currently trading at about 9.5–10 to the dollar for a year. You may be reading this a few years after publication, or there may be a devaluation (or overvaluation) of the peso. Exactitude in such things is self-defeating and constantly changing. I was fortunate that a real expert on the matter, John Bryant, of the **Mexico Retirement Travel Assn. (MRTA),** helped me with some of the information I do provide. His newsletter, *MRTA Newsletter* (P.O. Box 2190, Ste. 23, Pahrump, NV 89041) is invaluable for up-to-the-minute costs of living in Mexico. My own newsletter, *Latin America Travel & Business Report,* will help you with reports from expats throughout the country ($29.95 yearly; 1-800-321-5605, 1116 Ave. L, Galveston, TX 77550-6135). Canadians should join the Canadian Snowbird Assn., 180 Lesmill Rd., North York, Ontario M3B 2T5, Canada; 1-800-265-3200.

If you have to be concerned about every penny you will spend (and I am not putting you down—many people are on a very limited income and simply want the most for their money), then the only way to know what your own personal lifestyle will cost you is to go there. I strongly recommend you do that before tearing up your roots and moving. **Visit as a tourist for a couple of months, and try living in your chosen spot(s) for six** months to a year. I have been thanked for this advice more times than I can count. That doesn't mean that nobody I gave it to moved to Latin America. It means that some of them found out that it wasn't for them and saved themselves a lot of grief. Others found out that it was for them, but had a much better idea of what to expect when they made the move. Go. Enjoy. Live a little.

The Technical Stuff

Getting You and Your Stuff into the Country

Don't worry. You don't have to be a rocket scientist or a lawyer to understand this chapter. Mexico is so understanding that they will let either of the above into the country, as well as the rest of us. Getting into Mexico is simple. There are a few details that you need to take care of for your visit as a tourist. That is the way you should go the first time. **I do not recommend that you pack up everything and move to Latin America** without trying it on for size first. To do this, simply go as a tourist on a tourist visa and drive around for a while. Find a place you might want to live and stay there for a few months.

There is now a $15 fee to get a tourist permit. Your tourist permit (it's not really a visa—you don't need a visa to visit Mexico) is an FMT. It will be good for 180 days and all you have to do to get it is to prove that you are a citizen of some country. **NOTE: Border officials do not automatically offer the 180-day visa. Insist on it, saying that you want to tour all of Mexico.** You don't even have to prove that you are a good citizen. You'll need a passport or a birth certificate or a notarized statement of citizenship, along with a picture ID.

You can bring in a *reasonable* **amount of personal effects.** This varies according to the customs inspector. True, there is an official list of what is permitted, but it is seldom followed. As long as you do not have too much stuff, don't worry about it. Laptop computers are no problem. Desktops may cause you problems, especially at Arizona crossings. San Xavier Insurance will store yours. Duty is 20%. Sometimes you'll get them through, although you may be questioned about them. You will simply have to convince the customs official that the computer really is for your personal use and not for sale. You may end up paying a duty on your computer. There seems to be about a fifty-fifty chance of paying duty.

2

One time I was having a hard time with a computer until I told the official that I was a writer. "What kind of stories do you write?" he asked. "Like James Bond, 007." He beamed and waved me through. I have known people who have been turned back from one border crossing, who have driven to the next border crossing or waited for the shift to change and gotten in. New clothing with the tags still attached, even a couple of shirts, will almost always cause you trouble.

I might as well mention *mordida*, which means "a little bite." It is a *Mexicanismo* for bribe. It used to be a way of life on the border. The government periodically tries to stamp it out. In recent years, they have been more successful than before. Although I cannot encourage anyone actually to pay a bribe, and certainly don't suggest it, if an official makes it plain that there might be an easier way to deal with your situation, he is showing you that he is amenable to some token of appreciation for his extra services. At that point, you have to decide what you want to do. Under no circumstances should you offer anything without being encouraged. The new, young, idealistic crop of border officials will be insulted. I find it best to play by the rules, smile a lot and be friendly, but dumb.

Once, I had a new shirt with the tags on it and the customs officer at the secondary stop (approximately twenty-one kilometers from the border) insisted that I pay duty on it. I talked my way out of it by saying that my girlfriend thought I had such bad taste that she bought me a new shirt. Some of you may be saying, "Yeah, it's easy for him to say, he speaks Spanish. I don't." Most visitors to Mexico do not speak Spanish. Most customs officials speak some English and many are fluent. Don't worry about it. If you really want to learn Spanish, get the U.S. State Department Foreign Service Institute Language Course, sold in bookstores. There are a couple of companies that package it, but Multilingua is the least expensive. A great book for those who already know a little Spanish is *Breaking Out of Beginning Spanish* by Joseph J. Keenan (University of Texas Press).

Your Vehicle

To temporarily import your car, you need to obtain a **car permit** (cost $12). You will need to prove that you own it or are buying it. This means that you must have the title *or* registration, and a notarized letter of permission from the financing institution if it is financed. There was a bond of $400–$800 in effect for two days in December 1999. Thank God it was eliminated! See the story in my December 1999 newsletter at www.mexicomike.com/newsletters/Dec99/enter.htm (the password is "vol2."; this issue is offered free to readers of this book). So, if you read somewhere that you have to post a bond, ignore it. It is not true.

> *You will need a credit card, title or registration to your vehicle (or notarized permission from your lien holder) and a valid driver's license to get your car permit.*
>
> *You must have Mexican insurance. U.S. and Canadian insurance is not valid in Mexico.*

3

If your financing institution isn't familiar with this, have them call Nelson Insurance Agency (956-664-0670) and speak to the manager or claims adjuster. He will reassure them that the chances of its being stolen or involved in an accident are minimal and that, if it is, the insurance company will pay off. **You must have a credit card—VISA, MasterCard or American Express.** The Hacienda, or treasury department, will charge you an $11 fee to temporarily import the vehicle. **You cannot sell the vehicle in Mexico and must surrender this permit before you leave the country.**

You will need auto insurance. There was another recent shake-up in the Mexico insurance industry. There are two companies I can recommend from personal experience. Nelson Insurance Agency (no relation), 606 N. McColl, McAllen, TX; 1-800-906-7204, fax: 956-664-9608; e-mail: nmga@insurance mexico.com. I have known Charles Nelson, the owner, for years and have found him to be a straight shooter. San Xavier Insurance, Tucson and Nogales, AZ; 1-888-377-1570; www.mexican-auto insurance.com. The Acostas, who own the agency, are also excellent people to have on your side. Both have good rates and good service and will be there to pay a claim if you need them. Some of the other companies, which sometimes have "too-good-to-be-true" deals, may not be. You should also get a legal-assistance policy, which I highly recommend after having had an accident and used one.

AAA also sells Mexican auto insurance, but their prices are higher. Their Mexico guidebook is excellent, but you get that just by being a member. A California company that is reliable and has good rates is Adabis Global Insurance, P.O. Box 744, Temecula, CA 92593; 1-800-909-4457.

> *A left turn signal could be dangerous! Cows don't wear taillights.*

DRIVING IN MEXICO

Driving in Mexico is no more dangerous than driving in the United States, but it is more challenging. There are plenty of four-lane toll roads that (for a price) can make you feel as comfortable as if you were back home. The two-lane roads vary in width and conditions so that some of them are usually in great shape, and others are often full of potholes.

INTERNATIONAL DRIVER'S LICENSE AND SECOND PASSPORT

Forget the AAA ones. Mexican cops don't respect them. One company makes credit card–quality licenses with holograms that are very official-looking. You can get them in any name, from many countries. With one of these, you don't have to worry about surrendering your U.S. or Canadian license. Find out more about them from www.mexicomike.com or call 1-800-321-5605. A driver's license is only $120. A matching photo ID is $60. Both together are $135.

RULES OF THE ROAD

A left turn signal on the highway is used to tell the vehicle behind you that it is okay to pass you. In towns it means you are turning left. I worked for MTV as a driving consultant on their show *Road Rules.* One driver forgot that rule and the one about checking the side mirror before passing. Fortunately, we only lost a mirror. We could have lost much more.

Don't drive at night as there are often animals on the road. Cows don't wear taillights. Watch out for *topes* (speed bumps) in every town. They begin just as you enter a town and there are many in between. Slow down in rain—the roads are slicker, due to the blowoff from the big trucks, and it takes several hours of a heavy rain to wash it away.

Truckers are usually friendly and will use the aforementioned left turn signal to give you the go-ahead to pass when you cannot see around them. Traffic cops are more honest than you have been led to believe, but some are looking for bribes, especially in Mexico City. When this happens, stand firm and tell them you want to go to the *comandancia.* Mexico City has begun a program to eliminate corrupt cops, initially prohibiting all but female cops (considered to be more honest) from issuing tickets.

You can't drive in Mexico City on certain days, depending on the last number of your license plate (Mon., 5 or 6; Tues., 7 or 8; Wed., 3 or 4; Thurs., 1 or 2; Fri., 9 or 0). **This does not apply to rental cars. You will not go to jail for having a traffic accident,** unless you do not have insurance, are drunk or high or are argumentative. If the accident is serious, you could go to jail, or you and your car could simply be detained until the matter is settled. That's why it is a good idea to have a legal-assistance policy.

Flashing your headlights at a car in front of you indicates that you want to pass them. If you drive with your headlights on during the day, you will be flashed by oncoming drivers because they think you left them on by accident.

COPS

Corrupt cops are not as common as you think. In thirty years I have met four cops who tried to shake me down. Two succeeded. Most cops give tourists a break. I totaled my truck in Torreon. I did not go to jail, paid no bribes and was helped out by the officials of the toll road. The highway patrol was polite and efficient. They gave me a ticket for being stupid, and I had to pay for damaging the toll road, but that was it. Many times I have been lost (yes, it happens to the best of us) and a cop helped me on my way, refusing payment, saying, "I am only doing my job. Enjoy Mexico." I have heard ten of these stories for every bad-cop story—honestly.

There are corrupt cops on both sides of the border. Most of the stories you have heard are blown out of proportion. If a cop is corrupt, he is not out to hurt you, or rob you. He is merely looking for a privately financed pay raise. You have the power to grant that raise or not. You are the *patron.*

I do not mention the following to justify their actions, but so that you will understand the system. Local *transito* (transit) cops make about $100–$200 a month, depending on the town. *Policia Federal de Caminos,* Federal Highway Patrol, are the elite of the police forces and are well trained and well paid. Their salaries start at about $900 a month. They can make two times that with time and promotions. They do not stop people for shakedowns. Many of them are trained at the FBI academy in the United States. State cops, *judiciales,* are somewhere in between—in honesty, pay and courtesy. They have bad reputations. The federal judicial police, PJF, are what people call *Federales* and make $500–$600 a month. They are the villains of most horror stories. Mostly they are at drug checkpoints, wearing black T-shirts and baseball caps with PJF on the front.

5

They are very thorough and no-nonsense, but not terribly impolite. The army also mans drug and weapons checkpoints. They are usually polite and efficient. There is nothing to fear.

Now that I have given you the good news, I have to add that in some places local or state highway cops will shake down motorists. We gringos think this applies only to us, but we are not so unique. They happily shake down their countrymen. The states of Hidalgo and Mexico are noted for this, by my own personal experience and that of others. They will say you can't drive in their state on certain days. This is not true. The "day-without-a-car" program applies only to Mexico City, but cops will tell you differently. Argue the point. Mexico City cops used to be the worst, but Hidalgo and Mexico states aren't far behind.

If you are stopped, give the officer a **copy** of your papers and driver's license. This is when an international license comes in handy. If he is a scoundrel, he can't hold your papers hostage during the ensuing negotiations. Don't pay a bribe and do play dumb. If that doesn't work, say you want to go to the *comandancia y hablar con su jefe*. It is not perfect Spanish, and it is not supposed to be. Making it difficult to communicate is part of the game and one of your weapons. Stand firm for about thirty minutes and he will get disgusted and let you go. Always look for the officer's badge and write down his number, as well as the number of his patrol car. One lady, who was unjustly stopped, did this and the cop offered to trade her driver's license that he had illegally taken and documents for the paper with that information on it!

If you have really broken a law, the cop will take your license. You will have to appear at the police station or municipal offices to claim it by paying your ticket. On weekends, you will have to wait until Monday. You can drive with the ticket, but must return to appear by the appointed date. With legal-assistance insurance, you will be a lot better off. Get it. See more information at www.mexicomike.com. The legal system is slow and complicated. It even tried my patience the few times I have used it. If there is an easier way to handle the situation, find it.

Permanent Visas

Don't rush into getting one of these. Live there for a year or so and then decide whether you want to go through the bureaucratic maze necessary to obtain a more permanent visa. The requirements below are subject to change and they probably will. Do not take them as gospel.

FM-3 (THERE ARE THIRTEEN TYPES)

If you decide that living in Mexico is for you, then you will want to look into the requirements for an FM-3 visa, known as a *no inmigrante visitante.* The specifics will change from time to time, but as of press time, you will need a passport; two passport-sized pictures; a letter from the local police stating that you have good character (I know this would

Live in Mexico a year before you take the plunge. It is not for everyone. If you decide you like it, then you are ready to take certain legal steps like getting an FM-3.

be hard for me to produce); (I have been told that officially you need a medical statement proving you don't have HIV or anything else contagious, but I don't know anyone who has had to produce this); statements from your bank, broker or the company you retired from, or a copy of your social security statement proving that you have income of at least $800 a month, plus $400 per dependent. These amounts are halved if you own property and live in Mexico. If you are divorced, provide proof. The FM-3 visa costs $65 to get and $75 a year to renew. These requirements change frequently. Every Mexican consulate will give you different figures. In Mexico, FM-3s are easier to get. You can get one in Mexico and I recommend that. There, they welcome residents. In the States, they are prone to discourage you.

A few years ago the requirements were $1,230 per person. Now it is $1,100 per person, or $1,500 per couple, for U.S. citizens. For Canadians, the amount is less, depending on where you get the permit. Mazatlán is the easiest. Next week it could change again. Check with the local Mexican consul (not the tourist office) for the current requirements. If you own property in Mexico the dollar amounts are lowered. The FM-3 visa will entitle you to bring with you, without paying duty, your household goods, and technically, you will be freed from the necessity of renewing your car permit every six months like a tourist, but be wary. Not all cops and Hacienda officials are aware of this, and you may have to explain it to them if you are stopped for an expired permit. I have talked to people who have done just that and had no problems.

There is a debate about this. I have talked to expats and government officials who swear that, unless you pay an import tax, you will have to renew your permit every six months. Others (including government officials and other retirees) say you do not have to renew your car papers. They say that your car is legal as long as you are. They tell me they have been stopped by cops or Hacienda officials, and have shown them their FM-3s and been told they were okay.

My advice? It may depend on your locality. Most of the people who have told me that you don't need to renew the car papers lived around Chapala. Because this is subject to change (and perhaps interpretation), you should find out from other expats while you are in-country. What is without question is that you can come and go (even without your car) for the five-year period the visa is valid.

You do not need a lawyer to get your FM-3. In many areas of the country, particularly Guadalajara, the Gobernacion officials speak English. Again, if you are in the Guadalajara area, there is a fellow *paisano,* Ray Thornberry, who goes to the Lake Chapala Society and helps people with their forms for free.

Working in Mexico

It is possible to form your own corporation while you still have your FMT, or tourist permit. If you do, you will not be able to receive any pay from the corporation except for dividends or bonuses. You must hire Mexicans to work for you and you cannot work at the location of your business, although you can visit it to oversee the operations. Another way to work here is to marry a Mexican citizen and then put the business in his or her name and get him or her to hire you. Another way is to get yourself sponsored by a Mexican business and get hired. Then you can work, but only for that company. The smartest way to work is to get an FM-3.

For personal **advice about working in Mexico and setting up a corporation,** you can call me at 1-818-762-9333, or 1-800-321-5605, or contact me via e-mail at mexicomike@mexicomike.com. I have helped many people start successful businesses. I can save you hours of grief and frustration by giving you an honest evaluation of the ins and outs of setting up shop in Mexico. Subscribe to *Latin America Travel & Business Report* ($29.95 a year; 1-800-321-5605) for stories of those who have done it.

In fact, if you do plan to work in Mexico, you should also have a business plan and show the amount of money you are going to invest in the country when you make your application. The states of Sonora and Guanajuato are particularly open to foreign investment. The trick is not to open a business that is in direct competition with existing Mexican businesses, although this does not preclude you from doing so. The government is concerned that you aren't a freeloader who will be begging on the streets in six months and that you will pay taxes. By the same token, they don't want to put Mexicans out of work. The best way to keep up with the changing requirements is to subscribe to the *MRTA Newsletter*, P.O. Box 2190, Ste. 23, Pahrump, NV 89041.

Business Visas

There are many different flavors of FM-3s. For short business trips, get a free *visitante representante comercial*, good for thirty days at the border or airport.

If you are going to be there longer, or repeatedly, get the FM-3 business visa *(visitante hombre de negocios)*. Apply to any Mexican consul. You'll need a letter from your company saying why you are going. You must apply in person and present a passport, two passport-size pictures and a letter from your chamber of commerce, or articles of incorporation. It is valid for one year and costs $60. It entitles you to conduct business meetings, but not to work or earn wages in Mexico.

FM-3 for technicians—*visitante tecnico o cientifico*. Requirements are the same as above, plus you'll need a letter from your local police stating that you are not a criminal, and a letter from your company stating where you'll be working and that your company will be taking financial responsibility for you. Lastly, you'll need a letter from the Mexican company that is requesting your services. It costs $97.

The other types of FM-3s are *visitante: transacciones comercial, inversionista* (investor), *profesional, cargo de confianza, dependiente familiar, artista* or *deportista, consejero* (consultant), *estudiante, distinguido* (I will never get one of these) and last but not least, *ministro de cultura*. People traveling through Mexico to Central America need a *transmigrante* visa, or FMG. You only need to know about this if you are traveling expressly to Central America, particularly if you are bringing a lot of stuff with you. Requirements for this change, but you can expect to pay a fee of at least $150 and must produce a police letter stating that you are not a criminal and your car is not stolen.

FM-2

An FM-2 *(inmigrante rentista)* is like a green card, or resident alien card. It entitles you to many of the rights of a Mexican citizen (except voting) and entitles you to work. Officially, you must live in the country for five years, without working, and then make a *declaratoria de inmigrado,* and if it is approved, you can work. You will automatically receive this visa after five years of having an FM-3, if you also apply for it. It has certain drawbacks, such as only being able to drive a Mexican-plated car and a limitation on the time you can be out of the country. You must make an application to the Delegacíon de Gobernacíon. It costs $60 a year. My advice is to avoid getting this visa and go for the FM-3.

MISSIONARIES

You must have a special visa that entitles you to preach at a specific church. If you are caught preaching without one, you could be deported at the worst, or asked to leave town at the best. To get it, you must apply at a Mexican consulate, present the same documentation as for other visas and provide a letter from the church where you are going to preach. Also, I might mention that you should not plan on bringing down a lot of clothes or medicines unless you are willing to pay the customs duty on them.

Advice for Victims of Downsizing

You didn't ask for it. You didn't deserve it. You'd given your loyalty to a corporation and it gave you a pink slip. You may spend your next two years looking for a job (especially if you are over forty-five) and do nothing more than exhaust your savings and lose your home. Some of you will find jobs at lower pay, and life will be a struggle. You will learn to do with less.

WORKING IN MEXICO

Another, brighter scenario involves moving to Mexico. To do this, you will need some capital, as working is difficult (but not impossible) and it will take some time to go through the paperwork necessary to do so. If you have gotten a good-sized severance package, maybe you would rather "retire" early where it will cost less to live. The possibility of working in Mexico exists, though it will take perseverance and determination. I don't want to ncourage anyone to drop out, but if you feel like you've given it your best shot and aren't getting anywhere, what have you got to lose?

THE INTERNET

The simplest way to work in Mexico is to do so without setting up shop and have your money paid to you in the United States. If you are a consultant and can do much of your

So you want to be an importer? Advice from the Whip King of New Orleans—don't pin your hopes on goat fur, but if you do, don't let it get wet.

11

work by computer, then you can do it from Mexico, with an occasional commute. Indeed, with the Internet today, there's no reason why many of us can't operate from our homes, wherever they may be. Internet access is growing and is available in most of the larger towns. It is more dependable on the mainland than in Baja.

For personal advice on setting up a corporation or working in general, my friend Andy Sanders, 011-52-983-80404 at Xcalac, Q.R., is willing to act as a consultant for you for a reasonable fee. He really knows what he is talking about and can save you a lot of grief.

Another alternative is for those who can do some sort of seasonal work back in the States and live in Mexico in the off-season.

Many gringos work *off the books* in Mexico until they become legal. The drawback to that is if you get caught, you can be deported and everything you own can be confiscated. The likelihood of that happening really depends on where you are and how blatant you are about what you do. If you are in competition with a national and he gets jealous, he will turn you in. Therefore, do your best not to cross anyone. If you have made your *solicitud* for a working permit and it is in the works, you can usually operate. If your application is denied, close up shop right away. I have been told that work permits are harder to come by in the Baja.

If you teach English, you should have few problems, though you should have an FM-3. If you want to set up shop as an electrician or carpenter, forget it. If you do some sort of consulting work, you should get the *consejero* or *hombre de negocios* FM-3. I know people who work illegally and say that it is simply a matter of keeping a low profile and getting along with everyone. As it has recently been made easier to get an FM-3, why not go ahead and do it? Some people eke out a living driving cars to Central America to sell. There is nothing illegal about this, but it requires contacts and patience.

Recently, Costa Rica raised the duty, making it unprofitable. In other countries, you can make one-and-a-half times your money, but you must be patient. The people who want to buy cars know that you need money to live and will stall so you will lower your price. If you don't have deep pockets, they will win.

Importing handicrafts from Mexico or Central America is commonly done with a tourist visa. The chances of your getting caught are limited to traffic police. If they look in the back of your van and see several hundred *serapes,* they could make things sticky. Many people ship their packages back from Mexico via FedEx, Estafeta or DHL, or on the bus lines to avoid this. If you get stopped, a little *mordida* will usually do the trick. The cop doesn't really want a lot of Indian handicrafts, but he surely could use the money. Then it becomes a question of your bargaining ability. Decide in advance how much your load is worth to you. If you don't get stopped, keep that amount aside for another trip. Eventually, you will be stopped. Another good idea is to talk to U.S. customs officers and find out what is and is not duty-free. They will also tell you what paperwork is required to bring your treasures back.

From my own experience, I strongly advise you to talk to shop owners before you go and find out what they want. Don't fall in love with your own taste, even though it is probably a thousand times better than mine. I once cornered the market on goat-fur cushions because I thought they were unique. There was a reason I hadn't seen them in any stores—nobody wanted them. To add insult to injury, mine got wet. I don't know if you have ever smelled a wet goat, but I hope you don't have to. I never got the smell out of the upholstery of my first ex-wife's car—but that's another story, available in some of my other books. I was once the Whip King of New Orleans, but I only sold them. Don't ask, don't tell. Anyway, I found out what the market wanted and got a good deal on them. I am ashamed to admit it, but I also made a lot of money on velvet Elvises—something I never would have thought of on my own.

I recommend two books, *Born to Shop Mexico* by Suzy Gershman and Judith Thomas, and *The Shopper's Guide to Mexico* by Steve Rogers and Tina Rosa. The first concentrates on upscale shopping. The second is less likely to be out of date and covers marketplace shopping as well and gives you excellent explanations of the crafts of Mexico.

The Yin & Yang of Living in Mexico

I am not going to give you a glowing, hyperbolic report on living in Mexico that sounds as if it was written by a PR agent. I have lived for extended periods in Mexico and in and out of Central America for thirty years and once operated importing businesses selling goods from Mexico, Guatemala and Honduras. Subsequent editions of this book will include more information about Guatemala, Costa Rica and Honduras.

I love Mexico and Guatemala and believe that most of you will too. However, like a lover who has been in a relationship for many years, I have gone beyond the romance stage and see her for what she is.

She is still a beauty, but there are the inevitable flaws, some parts of her are sagging and some of the promises she made to an impressionable youth have not come true. I, of course, am not perfect either, but that is the subject of a much longer book. I will give you as honest an impression of the joys and headaches of living in Latin America as I can. You will have to make up your own mind. To do so, you will have to visit and see for yourself.

Most of this chapter deals with impressions of Mexico, but they apply equally to Central America. Each country of Central America is different, with a different flavor, but much of the Latin culture is universal enough to apply in a general way. Meanwhile, if a different Central American country is your destination, substitute the country of your choice for "Mexico" whenever you see it. I strongly suggest that you do not make up your mind about where you want to live until you have tried them all. Every country has its lovers and its detractors. There is no one paradise.

Over the last decade or so, I have gotten a reputation as an expert on Mexico and Central America. It has not gone to my head, as my father told me years ago that an expert was just a guy from out of town. He had intentions

> *May every Mexican you meet think you are the finest Americano he has ever known.*

of moving to Mexico in 1957. He was a forceful man, but a highly impractical one. My dear mother always went along with his flights of fancy and was always there to bail the family out when his flights crash-landed.

He packed up the car and headed South, to San Luis Potosí, capital of the state of the same name. I fell in love with Mexico then and there, as a young boy. I can't truly describe it, but with the colors, the smells, the warmth of foreign people who did not speak the same language, but who made me feel comfortable, I would have loved to move to Mexico.

My father, however, was typical of many who think they want to move there, but really aren't suited for it. He was a lawyer-turned-farmer. He had been drummed out of (or quit, no one is really sure) the legal profession in Chicago because of his inability to get along with people. He was a good farmer. He had a natural gift for it. He created new species of citrus fruits to improve his business. He was a man of few words, but expressed his love for my mother by creating new varieties of roses for her. He had a few friends and was not a bad man, but he became a different person in Mexico.

My father was the typical Ugly American. If you find yourself resembling him, do Mexico and yourself a favor and stay home. He refused to learn the language. Not only did he not learn Spanish, he expected everyone to speak English and said that the Mexican people all knew it and were refusing to speak it to him. He thought that if he shouted at them, they would respond better.

His plan to buy a ranch or farm (the two are used interchangeably in conversation) in San Luis Potosí came about because he had read a book written by someone who didn't know what he was talking about. It was well advertised and probably made a lot of money for the author. It resulted in a lot of people being disappointed. At a very early age, I was impressed with the power and the responsibility of the printed word. This book had told him that living in Mexico was easy, cheap and simple. It told him that he would be a king there, living on a pauper's income.

I noticed that the Mexican people were very quiet, almost shy and polite. Whenever my father spoke to them in his loud, authoritarian voice, they winced. Still, they were too polite to respond to him in kind. They were particularly offended when he said the name of their city. It is pronounced something like: Saan Louees Po toe seé, with an accent on the last syllable. He called it: San Louis Po **toé** see. It would have been an understandable mistake the first dozen or so times he did it, but after a few days, it became obvious that he had no intention of learning even the most basic politeness. He had gotten an invitation to meet the mayor. This man could have done wonders for easing my father's purchase of land, had my father merely been polite to the man. Instead, he corrected the mayor's halting English, shouted at him as if he were deaf or retarded and continually mispronounced the name of the man's city. My father was not a big man at city hall.

He referred to Mexicans (who are a very proud people and quite proud of their heritage) as Messkins, a loathsome south Texas term, or Indians, always said with derision. He was suspicious and always thought he was being cheated. He refused to learn how the peso worked. Instead, he paid for everything in dollars, asking, "How much is that in **real** money?" He got very drunk and abusive in the bar at the hotel. People talk about how unsafe a place Mexico is. How long do you think a foreigner with my father's attitude would have gotten along in the United States without someone taking a swing at him?

> *The difference between a glass half-full and a glass half-empty lies in the beholder, not the glass.*

He didn't know how to buy property in Mexico and just assumed (after all, he was a lawyer) that it worked the way it did at home. The best thing about the trip was that he didn't find any land he wanted, or he would have squandered our savings buying land from someone who probably didn't have the right to sell it to him.

When he returned, he was bitter toward Mexico and told all who would listen that they had better be careful when they went there, as he had been deep into the interior and knew what he was talking about. He was not unlike many of the people you will encounter when you say that you are considering moving to Mexico. After all, they have been there and they will tell you all the horror stories you can take. It is people like that who give the country a bad reputation. If you, who may never have been there, or may not have been outside the tourist enclaves of Acapulco, Cancún, etc., don't know any better, you will believe them. My father had been in the country of Mexico, but he never saw it. He never got beyond his own ego and misconceptions.

I was a child. I had no ego to speak of and no prejudices. I remember waiters smiling when I asked for Dr. Pepper and one who miraculously found one. I remember Mexican kids being like me, except for the language, and we played together and had a good time. I remember the warm days and cool nights, the air fragrant with wild, tropical scents. I remember the feeling of adventure and the kindness of everyone we met when they dealt with me. I also remember their unhappiness when they talked to my father, but they never took it out on me. After we left Mexico, I wanted to go back.

Both my father and I had been in the same place and had the same experiences. One of us loved the country and one of us hated it. Who was right? We both were. Mexico was not for my father. He would have been very unhappy there (in truth, he was unhappy anywhere he was, but that is another story). It is better that he did not move there, because after a few months or years, he would have had to leave and would have been able to blame his failures and unhappiness on the country.

I had a good experience and went back several times, eventually living there and now traveling there on a regular basis.

Some of you readers should not live in Mexico and some of you should not live anywhere else. You will not know just by reading this book. We are by nature self-deceiving. Although you might have all the character traits of my father, you probably won't admit it. Some of you won't know how you and Mexico will fit until you actually go and try it out. Mexico is more than a place. It is a state of mind. It affects people differently. In the past decade, I have seen thousands of people come through my office seeking advice about traveling and living in Mexico.

I remember one fellow from Boston who had an expensive motor home and was the most uptight man I had ever met. He had his wife, children and grandmother with him. He was so filled with apprehension and worry about his expensive motor home that I told him that he should just not go.

He was taken aback. "I thought your job was to encourage people to go to Mexico." "No," I replied, "my job is to help people to have a good time and you are so worried about your motor home that you will not have a good time. Do us both a favor and stay home." He thought about it and said, "What if I leave the motor home here and just take the car?" He did, and his two-week trip became a monthlong journey of self-discovery. I saw him when he returned and he was completely relaxed and smiling.

I have a place to stay if I ever get to Boston (and find his address, which I have lost). That experience taught me that I should never judge whether someone will fit into Mexico, but I can make general assumptions about what might not work. Follow your heart, but take some of my suggestions to the same place.

You'll Do Fine in Mexico or Latin America If:
You have a spirit of adventure.

Even if you are going to live in Mexico City and work for a company, life will be an adventure. You can either have fun with it or be frustrated by it. The choice is always yours.

You are not anal-retentive.

If you think everything has to be in its place and there must be a logical explanation for everything, then you are going to spend a lot of time unhappy. Learn to "go with the flow."

You are willing to accept things as they are.

There's a wonderful little prayer that says in part, "God, grant me the serenity to accept the things I can't change, courage to change the things I can and the wisdom to know the difference." You may find yourself repeating this when little "Mexicanisms" get between you and getting things done. You will find yourself using it less in Costa Rica.

You truly like people.

Remember that you are never alone in Latin America. Even if (especially if) you live in a small town where there are no other gringos, you will meet many locals. They are a gregarious bunch with large families and a healthy curiosity about the bizarre ways of foreigners. Remember that many of the things we take for granted about ourselves are pretty darned amazing to outsiders. Old people and small kids will ask you questions as you travel about. Middle-class businessmen will go out of their way to help you when you need it. Strangers of all classes will show you things and help you find whatever it is you are looking for, be it a road out of town or a battery for your car alarm.

You have a sense of humor.

This is probably the most important ingredient in enjoying life in Latin

America. If you do not take yourself too seriously, you will do much better than if you do. If you are a very serious or sad person and you have been sent to Latin America by your company, take heart—your whole personality could change for the better.

Those are the main personality traits that will make your life in Latin America easier. I'm not a psychologist (I'm afraid of what I might find out if I visited one), and there is absolutely nothing scientific about my list. It is based on my experience and what I have gathered from the thousands of people I have talked to and observed over the last several years. It is only to give you an honest assessment of some of the differences of living in Mexico.

What to Expect

First of all, I would like to say that, although many people think prices are the reason they want to move to Mexico, I suggest that it is something else. There is a sense of freedom, or rediscovering yourself, that motivates many of us to live away from the comfort and security or our own country. We are looking for a better way of life. We may be sick of the harsh winters of our homeland, of the crime and constant living in fear or merely of the constant sameness that deadens our souls. No matter what our reason for wanting to try life in another country, we must first be motivated to leave. After we have passed that hurdle, we must then begin to think of the practicalities, of the cost of living.

Of course, if you have a very limited income and are barely making it in the United States, then you want to be sure that you are not jumping out of the frying pan into the fire. Also, you may be an artist who wants to get away to write your book or paint your pictures. You have saved a certain amount of money and think you can survive for a year if you watch your pennies, so knowing exact costs is important to you. To both of you, I recommend that you look at this as an adventure and realize that you are not going to be able to predict costs to the penny. By the same token, you will find yourself setting a budget and finding a way to live on it.

Almost everything will be cheaper in Latin America, but not as cheap as you have been led to believe. At the moment, with the peso having devalued from 3 to the dollar to between 9.5–10 to the dollar, living in Mexico is cheaper than it has been in years. Guatemala is a little more expensive than it has been in the past, but still cheaper than Mexico. Costa Rica is the most expensive of the lot, and always has been. These factors could change in a heartbeat with a sudden devaluation, intense inflation or other factors beyond anyone's control.

QUALITY OF LIFE

What's more important is that your quality of life **will be better**. If you come from the Frozen North (as I call everywhere north of Texas), you will be getting away from the biting cold that demoralizes you and makes your joints ache. You will be getting away from a siege mentality that affects so many of us who live in cities. You will be getting away from your boring neighbors who are afraid to take any chances in life. You will be getting to a place where you can find yourself and enjoy life again.

CHILDREN

If you have children, you will be able to relax more here. I can't think of anything better than being a kid in Mexico. They have more freedom. You don't have to worry about weirdos and depraved creeps who will kidnap or molest your kids. It is not unusual to see Mexican kids in the town square at ten o'clock at night. This might not be true in the larger cities, but it is true in most places. It would be irresponsible of me to say that nothing bad ever happens in Mexico. It does, but not with the frequency that it does in the United States. Many people worry about *banditos* and being robbed. I frankly have more fear in the United States than I do in Mexico. This has been validated by the thousands of foreigners who live there. Forget the negative things you read in the press. Their job is to make news. It doesn't make news if 7,999,999 tourists had a great time. If one has a bad time, now **that's** news.

Medical Care

Medical care is a reasonable concern. You will find doctors and dentists and hospitals to be a good deal cheaper in Latin America, but you will probably have to pay for them yourself. Although there are special insurance policies for expatriates, Medicare and your average insurance

> *Medical care is less expensive than in the States. Most prescription drugs are available. Medicare is not valid though this may change soon.*

company will ignore your claims. Some folks have told me that their stateside insurance will pay claims incurred in Latin America, but these insurance companies are very specific about what paperwork they accept and then only pay a part of the claim. Canadians have a special situation and it varies from province to province. Medipac International (180 Lesmill Rd., North York, Ontario M3B 2T5, Canada; 1-800-563-5104, fax: 416-441-7010) offers out-of-country insurance. They are endorsed by the Canadian Snowbird Assn.

If you have a high deductible, you may find out that it is unlikely that you will ever reach it, unless you are really seriously ill. I would never advise anyone to drop their medical coverage, but you should make sure that it will pay off for you. You should also consider that you may elect to return to the States for treatment, and then, brother, you'd better have some kind of coverage. Check with your insurance carrier before you go.

There is an excellent international medical air evacuation available from MEDEX, 1447 York Rd., Ste. 410, Lutherville, MD 21093. Many auto insurance companies also offer air evacuation insurance to their customers. It is worth it.

There are also a lot of unscrupulous outfits that offer great deals, but don't pay off. Please investigate thoroughly before you spend your money for any medical or air evacuation plan. Ask how long they have been in business, get references and check with the state they are licensed in, as well as with other expatriates. It's probably wise to get some kind of health insurance coverage on the way down, while you are investigating the area. American International Underwriters and International Services of America (401 N. Alma School Rd., #9, Chandler, AZ 95224; 1-800-647-4589 or 602-821-9052, fax: 602-821-9297; www.abilnet.com) both offer it.

Lab tests will cost about a third of what they do here. The work is generally good. I know many people who swear by them and have no desire to spend three times as much back home. Dental work is absolutely fantastic. Many "Winter Texans" flock to Mexican dentists across the border to have everything from fillings and cleanings to plates and dentures done. The cost is less than half of the cost in the United States.

Medical doctors still make house calls ($20) and are very good. In fact, many have trained in U.S. hospitals. Many U.S. doctors have in fact trained in Mexican medical schools, notably in Guadalajara. They are more prone to diagnose by feeling and touching than to require extensive lab tests, but they will order tests when necessary. Even in small towns, good *medicos* are available. Although they may not speak English in a small town, I have heard nothing but good reports from those who have used them (including me). Hospitals are adequate and some are quite good and well respected. Some perform open-heart and transplant surgery. Your doctor can advise you whether you are better off returning home for whatever ails you or getting it done there.

Nursing care in hospitals is less than perfect. Try to have a family member get instructions from the doctor on what follow-up care is needed and have them there to make sure his orders are followed. If you have serious medical conditions that require special equipment, you should think twice about moving, although this is changing rapidly.

Dialysis is a good example. A few years ago, I would have told you to be wary of living in Latin America if you require dialysis, based on my friends who came to McAllen for treatment from Mexico. Now you will have no problems in the major cities of Mexico. Some U.S. hospital chains are moving into Mexico and setting up modern facilities with well-trained staffs. I suspect that the situation can only get better.

You can avail yourself of inexpensive medical care by joining the national health care system, IMSS. It costs $255 a year. Applications are accepted in January, February, July and August. There is a six- to-nine-month waiting period.

DRUGS, LEGAL

Most prescription drugs are readily available from the same manufacturers that produce drugs in the Unted States and that have plants in Mexico. They will often cost less than half of what they do in the United States. One thing I should warn you about is that the dosage is sometimes different than what you are used to—higher concentrations of the main ingredient, for example. Creams are often combined with different ingredients than what you got back home.

Take a copy of the *Physicians Desk Reference* or *The Pill Book* or some other book that describes in detail the effects of the interactions of all drugs. If you take a lot of prescription drugs, you could save a fortune buying them in Mexico. Just make sure that you are getting exactly the dosage you want. It is not hard to read the labels and many pharmacists speak English. Discuss your needs with them and don't let them sell you something that you don't really want.

There are some exceptions. Certain drugs needed by **hemophiliacs,** for example, are unavailable. My advice is to come down with a goodly supply of whatever drugs you regularly take, find a physician and discuss your medical needs.

Theoretically, you could get the information on drug availability before you go, but I have never been able to find a reliable source. The best way is to go and find out for yourself. I'm not passing the buck here. It's just a key fact about Latin America. Many things you will not figure out without a personal visit. If you have access to a hospital or university with a good tropical medicine department, they should be able to refer you to someone who is familiar with where you are going and who can give you a better idea of your prospects for finding the medication you need. That's another thing about living in Latin America. It's pretty darn hard to get accurate information before you go. Things change so much and so often that it is impossible to keep up. Take everything with a grain of salt and get the real scoop when you get there. Other expatriates are usually your best sources of information.

DRUGS, ILLEGAL

Don't. I know that those of you who want to use them will, but try to focus (as hard as that can be when you want to get high) on the fact that if you get caught, you will immediately go to jail and be found guilty. There are drug checkpoints on every highway and the enforcement officers use dogs. Your chances of getting caught and prosecuted are greater in Mexico than in the United States—even for small amounts. I know of one case where a trio of college students was arrested for having too many Valium they had bought legally at pharmacies. If you do get caught, see if you can resolve the situation immediately. If not, do not start shelling out money to a jailhouse lawyer recommended by one of your keepers. You have the right to contact the U.S. or Canadian consul and you should do so. Although the consular officer will not get you out of jail, he or she will give you a list of recommended lawyers. They are more reputable than most.

Communications

TELEPHONES AND OTHER FAIRY TALES

First of all, this is changing rapidly, and for the better. Meanwhile, expect things to operate differently than they do back at home. When you rent or buy a habitat, make sure that the phone comes with it. Seriously. I don't mean the physical instrument (you can use your own, providing you have one that is switchable from tone to pulse, as pulse is the norm in Mexico), but the actual line and connection to the phone company.

When you see a line of people at a pay phone, get in line. Surely there is someone you need to call. Get a phone card.

Getting new phone service is theoretically possible and I have known people who have done it, but the usual scenario is that it takes ages.

There are *casetas de larga distancia* (long-distance offices) in every city, hamlet and truck stop where you can have a real, human operator place a call (or send a fax) for you. Doesn't that take you back in time? They are great fun and you should try one just for the heck of it.

You will have to have a prepaid phone card to use most of the newer phones. Fortunately, they are available just about everywhere, from convenience stores to gas stations. Not all public phones work. When you see a line of people standing by a phone, get in line. There is directory assistance in Mexico, but don't count on it. I must always call when the operator is on a siesta. Calling home can be expensive unless you call collect or use a calling card like ATT, MCI or Sprint. Mexicans will always give you a telephone number with "01" as the first two digits. This is the code to dial long distance inside Mexico. To dial into Mexico from outside, you must dial "011" (for international access), then "52" (the country code for Mexico), then the area code, then the local phone number.

LATE-BREAKING NEWS ON PHONE SERVICE

There's a new deal in phone service that could save you a bundle. But first, a little background. Already there are seven U.S. companies primed to offer long-distance phone service in Mexico in partnership with Mexican companies. On January 1, 1997, they charged into the country like sailors on shore leave heading for an ice cream parlor (or wherever sailors go). This

To dial Mexico from the States, dial "011-52" + the area code (2 or 3 digits) + the phone number (5 to 8 digits). Inside Mexico dial "01" + the area code + the phone number.

should only help the consumer, but there may be a few bad deals. Remember what happened when dozens of long-distance carriers started taking over the public phones in this country?

The giant TelMex (Telefonos de Mexico) is in partnership (10%) with SBC/Southwestern Bell and Sprint. Unicom is partly owned by GTE. Alestra (no relation to the fat substitute that sounds the same) is owned by Grupo Alfa (51%) and the rest is owned by AT&T. MarcaTel SA is really international. The Mexican company Radio Beep is in partnership with U.S. companies: IXC Communications, Westel and the Canadian company Teleglobe. Iusatel is owned by Bell Atlantic (41.9%) and the Mexican cellular company Iusacell SA. Investcom is wholly owned by Grupo Comunicaciones San Luis SA. All this means that there will be tremendous competition and improvement in the phone market.

Avantel, a joint venture between the Mexican Grupo Finaciero Banamex and MCI, has switching facilities in Guadalajara, Mexico City and Monterrey. Besides long-distance service (and phone cards) they offer Internet services. They plan 20,000 kilometers of fiber optics and now have about 5,000 kilometers of fiber optics.

Beware of MCI, Sprint and other calling cards. They have been known to offer one rate over the phone and another when you get home. A friend of mine got stuck for a $1,000 phone bill because the rate promised had tripled when actually charged. Be sure when you get a phone card that the rate quoted is for calling from Mexico to the States or Canada.

There is one company that offers good calling rates from residential phones inside Mexico. It is Telegroup. I like them so much that I advertise them on my web page, www.mexicomike.com.

With so many companies offering phone cards in the United States, I should warn you that they are *not all reputable.* There have been cases where their rates were higher, or they had inadequate switching facilities. Buyer beware.

CELLULAR PHONES

These are everywhere. No self-respecting Mexican businessman would be without one. The great Zamba once had two. There is no prohibition against your taking a cellular phone into the country. If a customs inspector tells you otherwise, insist that he show you the law prohibiting it. I have hardly ever heard of anyone having any trouble. Check with your cellular carrier here to get the access numbers for the cities where you will want to use it.

FAX MACHINES

Get a fax machine. This is the most reliable way to communicate and it is cheaper than calls back to the States or Canada, as you can send your faxes in the middle of the night and they are usually shorter than conversations. When you are sending a fax to Mexico, don't just put something in your machine and expect it to go through. Most (and again this is changing) small businesses and some fairly good-sized companies still use the fax line for voice. You must wait for a human being to answer and ask them, *"Quisiera el tono de fax, por favor."* I have a nifty fax/phone answering gadget in my computer and a fax machine that also is an answering machine. I have found that my computer fax does not always accept calls from Mexico, but the stand-alone unit does. I don't know if it is a quirk in my fax/modem or if it is a common problem. You should have no trouble getting a fax machine through customs, provided it is not in the box and looks a little used. Spit on it or get your kids to put greasy fingerprints on it.

MAIL

This is one area that is changing slowly. Mexican mail service is slow and unpredictable. Most Mexicans pay their utility bills in person for that reason. You should too. If you want something to get where it is going and not take an extended vacation to Chiapas or Chihuahua, send it (within the country) by Estafeta, DHL, FedEx or one of the other courier services. UPS has a small presence in Mexico, but so far they have not been as reliable. Ask other expats whom they trust. You can also send it by Mexpost, a service of the Mexican postal service. I have used it nationally and internationally and have been amazed at the speed with which my packages have been delivered. Maybe I should have said "pleasantly" amazed. If you are sending a package, use the bus system.

If you are sending mail to Mexico from the States, put the *codigo postal* (zip/postal code) *in front of the town where it is going.* Putting it at the end almost guarantees that some of it will embark on a journey to Sri Lanka or darkest Africa—no foolin'. Don't forget to put "MEXICO" in caps at the bottom of your address. For mail sent within Mexico put the *codigo postal* where it belongs. Until you get an address, you can have mail sent to you in care of yourself at the *lista de correos,* or general delivery. Have your correspondent write your name, *lista de correos, codigo postal,* city, state, MEXICO. Be sure to write *Correo Aereo* on the envelope for airmail. I have had mixed luck sending packages back to the United States, but be sure to write "unsolicited gift" on the outside, so your receiver does not have to pay duty. Expect that the package will be inspected.

For getting mail to and from the States and Canada, most towns with any gringo residents have a mail drop where you can deposit your mail and pick it up. These businesses have couriers who run to the States regularly. They are your best bet for paying bills and keeping up your correspondence. If you can arrange to have your bills paid directly from your U.S. bank account and have your checks deposited there, that is the best bet. For communicating with the folks back home (if only to "dig them" [which in Spanish slang is *chingale,* although it really has a much worse meaning, so be careful when using it] about the wonderful weather you are enjoying while they are shoveling snowdrifts), use the Internet.

COMPUTERS AND THE INTERNET

There is a growing Internet presence in Mexico. Almost daily, some new city is brought online. There are Internet providers springing up like wildflowers after a summer rain. They always advertise in the English-language papers and the local papers, so you should have no problem finding one. CompuServe is also strong in mainland Mexico, but not the Baja. America Online has a tiny presence. Avantel has a good setup with MCI.

I should add one caveat to the joys of telecommuting, however. Although Internet access from the mainland is pretty dependable, it depends on where you are. I understand that from the Baja, it is less dependable. Costs vary from locale to locale, depending on the competition, but you can figure about $20–$30 monthly for twenty hours. My sources in the Baja inform me that connections there are not very dependable. On the mainland, most people tell me that, although there are more glitches than here, the situation is improving. I correspond with many people from Mexico and, overall, it seems to work.

Whatever you do with your computer, be sure to buy a good surge protector and/or a UPS. Isotel makes good ones and they are reasonably priced. Some of their models even guarantee against lightning strikes. They have a lifetime guarantee for damage of your computer equipment for up to $25,000. I did not ask them if this applies outside the United States and Canada. Even if it doesn't, it seems like they offer pretty hefty protection. Don't just get one of those cheapie power outlets. You need something that has instantaneous response time and a 1,500-joule (or better) spike suppression. Get one with modem protection. There are few three-pronged plugs, so get an adapter at a hardware store that converts three prongs to two.

Power outages and brownouts occur, as does dropping power followed by a surge. Many people use surge protectors for their TVs, stereos and VCRs as well. It is certainly a wise precaution. Be sure to back up your hard drive religiously. You can get many computer supplies in the larger cities. Mexico is a very technocratic society. I personally prefer a stand-alone fax machine for receiving calls. You will also need it to send a variety of documents, so get one, even if you have a fax/modem.

Banking

Your best bet is to open an account with the California Commerce Bank, 615 S. Flower St., Los Angeles, CA; 213-624-5700. They have a deal called the "Programa Amistad" that enables you to access your money in Mexico through Banamex, of which they are a subsidiary. They have a Mexican phone number that is toll-free: (remember what I told you a few pages back? This was a test to see if you are reading carefully) (91) 800-90-225. In general, I have found Mexican banks to be a royal pain in the patoot. There are endless lines and overwhelming bureaucracy. You will typically stand in the wrong line four or five times before you catch on—or at least I did. And this was just to cash a traveler's check.

This is changing because the banks have been sold to private investors and they are beginning to learn what customer service means, but it will take a while. Allen W. Lloyd offers banking and investment services for foreigners. Promex is a popular bank in the Guadalajara area and deals with a lot of foreigners. Other good banks are Banamex and Bancomer. A good friend told me how happy he is with his bank in Acapulco. There is an officer he deals with on a first-name basis and she speaks English. So just scout around and maybe you will find a good Mexican bank that treats you right.

If you deposit a U.S. check, count on fourteen days before you can use the money. A Mexican check can take from three to ten days to be credited. Then the banks (all of them) nickel-and-dime you to death with incomprehensible service charges. You certainly don't want to borrow any money from them as interest rates, which vary, are currently around 70%! During the crisis of 1995, they were as high as 140%! Of course, the other side of that coin is that you can garner some hefty interest on your own shekels by getting a *cuenta maestra,* which pays you interest and allows you to write checks and use a debit card.

My friend in Acapulco, Tom Alexander, was able to pay for his daughter's wedding from the interest on his account—about 37% at the time. There are also straight certificates of deposit for time periods of 30–180 days. There is a risk, of course, of a devaluation where, like many Mexicans, you could wake up with your pesos being worth one-half of what they were the night before. **I ain't giving you any financial advice.**

The easiest way to get money is to use your debit card from your home bank at an ATM machine. These are everywhere. Cirrus is the most popular, followed by Pulse. Plus is sometimes accepted. You can also use your VISA or MasterCard for cash advances at the ATM. If you go to a bank to use them, you will have to show a passport. You know, of course, that there is a hefty fee for the service. Unfortunately, ATMs in smaller towns always seem to be out of cash. If you have an American Express card, you can go to any American Express office and get up to $500 in AMEX traveler's checks.

EMERGENCY MONEY

You can get money sent to you by Western Union, and it can be picked up in a matter of minutes at 2,700 locations from telegraph offices or 400 Electra department stores, open from 9 A.M. to 9 P.M. Western Union charges the sender about 10%. You lose another 10% at your end. It's fast, but expensive. Your best bet is to have a friend deposit the money in your home account and retrieve it via an ATM.

> *There is more than one way to skin a cat or get emergency money in a hurry.*

International U.S. Postal Service money orders are honored, and this is how most Mexicans working in the United States send money back home.

Bancomer signed a deal in May 1996 so that you can transfer money from U.S. post offices in California and Texas to their 900 branches in Mexico.

Wells Fargo has a deal with Banamex whereby someone in the United States opens an account for an annual $10 fee and then pays $10 for each wire transfer. Banamex automatically opens an account for the recipient. The transfer can take from a day (unlikely) to five days at the outside.

A simple bank-to-bank transfer will cost about $45 and take between one and three days.

My personal advice while you are just traveling around, looking for your spot to land, is to take about $600 in cash, $1,000 in traveler's checks and use the ATM card for anything else. Don't bother with the aggravation of a bank to change money. Use a *casa de cambio,* or exchange house (like a *bureau de change* in Europe). These independent businessmen have stands in every town of any size. Find one that does not charge a commission. In small towns, I have changed money at hardware stores and pharmacies. On the road, I have gotten varying rates at Pemex gas stations.

Living There—
Costs in General

Retirement Communities

There is an interesting process going on in Mexico now. Some developers have begun building entire communities for foreign retirees, mostly American and Canadian "snowbirds." These escapees from the cold winters have found that Florida is too expensive for them and still want to live in a pleasant climate. This sort of living is not for everyone, but it is welcome news to many retirees who want the security and ease of living in a community of people like themselves. In most of them, houses range from about $25,000 to $80,000.

I must offer a word of **caution**, however. Mixed among the **good guys** are some **bad guys.** The retirement market is booming, similar to the land craze that swept Florida in the 1950s. A lot of people made some pretty good deals there, but a lot more got taken. I don't want to be in the least bit responsible for anyone's grief, so I will err on the side of caution in mentioning these communities. There are some unscrupulous scam artists. They sell trips to their locations as "retirement and investment planning" tours to Mexico. Beware.

Some of these outfits are perfectly legitimate. I can only mention a few because I do not know about them all. If I do not mention a development, that does not necessarily mean it is suspect. You should, however, exercise due diligence in investigating any of them, **including the ones I mention.**

One thing I should warn you about is that some developers will offer familiarization trips to their developments and offer to discount your purchase price by enough to pay for your trip to encourage you to buy from them. There is nothing wrong with this and it is a good deal *if* you decide that that particular development is for you.

Let me give you an example of how these "free" airfare deals work. There was a developer in Chapala who offered his property (not yet developed) for $69,900. A few weeks later, he was in Canada and offered the same property for $79,900 (U.S.), but that included airfare and hotel. Gosh, did he fly them there in the Concorde? Of course, the "free" airfare and hotel was only applicable if the prospect bought property.

In Ajijic, Jalisco, there is a developer named Jaimie Hernandez who is highly recommended. He has three developments under his belt: Mission del Lago (28 homes), Lomas del Lago (49 homes) and Lomas de Ajijic (32 homes). His latest development is Villas San Andres (six homes). His next is an ambitious plan called Ajijic Country Club and Spa. He plans to have a nine-hole golf course, spa with Jacuzzi, massage, sauna, etc., a club house, tennis courts, heated pool and more. His lots will range from $60,000 for 7,000 square feet to $130,000 for 11,000 square feet. He estimates the cost of construction to be about $44–$48 per square foot. Houses should cost about $90,000–$180,000. Many of the people I talked to in the Guadalajara/Chapala area spoke highly of him. His phone/fax in Ajijic is (011-52-376) 6-2104.

The days of living in luxury for $300 a month are long gone. You can, however, live on less in Mexico than in the United States or Canada. I have talked to a number of people who still live on $300–$500 a month, but they do not live in gringo communities and they are frugal.

There are a number of developers in the retirement business. I have not investigated all of them. I do know of one or two that are questionable and will not mention them. The rest may be perfectly legitimate, but I am not going to mention any deal that I do not believe to be legitimate.

Another development I know to be legitimate is in Valle de Bravo, near Toluca, Mexico, called Avandaro. It is not a retirement community per se, but it is a very nice development of high-class homes in a beautiful setting. It also is a golf-course development.

My advice is not to leave your common sense in your other suitcase. If a development has to use high-pressure salesmen to get your business, then

Good news for those on a budget.

look elsewhere. Don't make any rash decisions. Ask the local expatriate organizations what their opinion of the development is.

Be sure to find out if the developer really has a clear title to the property it is selling. A representative should be able to show you a deed clear of encumbrances, signed by a notary public. Then you should be able to consult with that notary to make sure that it is legitimate. **Before you buy any piece of property in Mexico, have a notary public check it out.** Get an English-speaking notary. You don't have to rely on the developer's notary, if you don't feel comfortable. If the company is on the up-and-up, it should have no objection to review by an independent notary. Lawyers are handy for certain things, but only a notary public can tell you if something is truly unencumbered.

What some developers are hoping to do is to get enough capital from people like you, so that they can continue their development and actually buy the property they are developing. If it doesn't work out, well, gee, they will be very sorry, but you will be the one left holding the bag. Remember, if something is a good deal today, it will be a good deal next week. It is not the stock market.

Although specific prices are subject to change, you should be aware of one very important thing. The days of being able to live in luxury in Mexico for $300 a month are over. Most people should figure that it will cost about 70–80% of what it costs them to live in the States (and perhaps 10–15% less in Guatemala; Costa Rica living costs will be very close to those in the United States). Now, that being said, I'll go out on a limb. Because some of you will be younger people seeking an artistic life and a place to hide away and write that novel or paint your masterpiece, or older people on a small Social Security check, don't despair.

It is possible to live in Mexico (or the other countries) for less—if you are willing to do without a lot of creature comforts and live more like a local than a foreigner. I do have to be negative for a moment, or my conscience won't let me sleep. If you are one of those people who exists solely on a Social Security check of $450 a month, *please read this caveat.* You will be able to live in Mexico (many Mexicans don't make that much), but you will have to be frugal.

You will have to rent a smaller apartment rather than a house and must be willing to learn how to live like the local middle-class people. You may find it is a wonderful life and be extremely glad you made the change, but it is not for everyone. You will not be able to live in luxury with a maid, etc. If you still want to try it, forsake the gringo communities and check out some out-of-the-way locales. I do know some young-at-heart people who live in Mazatlán and Morelia (and other places) for under $200 a month. I also know people who live there who swear you can't survive for under $900 a month. Both are correct. It all depends on how you want to live. You might also consider Guatemala, which is less expensive than Mexico.

33

I lived in Pto. Escondido, Oaxaca, in 1983–1984 on $120 a month. My lifestyle was simple and I did without a lot. My rent and utilities were about $90. I bought fresh fish from the local fishermen in the morning. I ate veg- etables. I slept on a cot, but I did have *My personal adventures, before and after living in Mexico.* an electric fan over it. My showers were cold (which kept my libido in check). After a few months, I lent my landlord some money and he bought a refrig- erator. My stove was two propane burners. My entertainment budget was two Cokes or coffees a night—and I went to the local no-charge, dirt-floor disco every night. This was during a time when sane people could have lived in Mexico for $300 a month.

By way of comparison, in 1984–1985, I moved to Seattle, Washington, and lived there for $160–$180 a month. In Seattle, I shared a house and spent $110–$120 a month on rent and utilities, versus the $90 I spent in Mexico. I ate a diet of strictly rice, beans, potatoes, popcorn and jalapeños with occasional ice cream at twenty-five cents a gallon for a treat. The only meat or fish I ever ate was given to me. I walked most everywhere but still took the occasional bus. I spent a lot of postage sending my stories out to heartless editors.

Where was my life fuller? In many ways it was richer in Mexico. There I did not feel as poor. In Seattle, I felt that I was paying my dues to write better, but I can't say that it was fun. Of course, I had access to a library, a postal system that worked and telephones. I left Mexico consciously, because I had done all I could do there. It is easy to write in Latin America. It is hard to sell your stuff if you are not already well established.

I returned to both of my old stomping grounds a year before the devaluation. In Pto. Escondido, the same one-room house is now part of a small condo development called "Villas Santiago." They rented for $350.

Food prices had gone up. At the time, I figure I could have lived there under the same conditions for about $450 a month. Now, with the devaluation (despite the ensuing inflation), I could live there for about $350. Next year, who knows what it will cost? There are cheaper places to rent on the beach, for about $200 a month, but they have community cooking facilities, using wood fires. My friend Joe King Carrasco lived in one of them and wrote some mighty fine songs while he was there. That's not really a bad thing and you would probably meet a lot more people that way. The toilets would be communal and the showers would be cold. It all depends on how you want to live. For two people living together, add about 40%.

> *To really live cheaply, look for a small town.*

In Seattle, my same room rents for $250 a month and utilities have gone up about 30%. Food prices have gone up. Bus prices have gone up. I figure that I could live there for about $400 monthly today. I could live in Pto. Escondido under Spartan conditions for about $300 a month and in Seattle for about $100 more. I would eat better in Mexico, the weather would be nicer and I would meet a wider variety of friends, but they would all be transient. Please remember that this is rock bottom budget. True, there are hippie couples who would call that luxury, because they would be paying a dollar or two to sling a hammock, but it's as rock bottom as I would want to get—and I don't want to today.

If you moved down the road to Pto. Angel, you could save hundreds a month by living in a thatched-roof hut. As you can see, if you want to be really bohemian, you can still live relatively cheaply in Mexico. And if you are making minimum wage at some grunt job, you are making twice what you would have in 1983, so you should be able to save some money and do it.

That's the bare-bones way to live. If you do it, you will have to do without a phone, a daily newspaper and lots of eating out (and if you do, you'll have to eat at starkly local eateries). Forget calls home, new clothes, impulse buying and medical care. Of course, you will almost be living like a lot of Mexicans. The difference is that you will not have a family structure to fall back on.

The Good News

Now, if you are middle-aged or better, either in body or spirit, it's another story. If you want to live comfortably, in a community that has a few gringos, you will probably have to spend about $800–$1,500 a month.

You will have a phone, hot and cold running water, a decent bed and you will be able to eat out occasionally (though you will have to get good value for your money). You will be able to afford medical care (at additional cost). For two people living together, add about 50%. Yes, I know this is higher than the first reference, but when you have two people who are not living so close to the edge, they are both more likely to splurge occasionally. I know couples who live on $600–$900 a month, but they work at it.

If you choose to live in a small town, for example, Montemorelos, Nuevo Leon, you could rent a simple house for around $100–$150 a month and get a part-time maid for another $20. Of course, you would have to be independent in spirit to live there, as there will be few other gringos for company. This same information applies to just about any small town without a large foreign community. For some, this might be a perfect solution if your income is small and you don't need a lot of social life with other gringos. You would be forced to learn Spanish and could assimilate into the Mexican community if you wanted to. It could be a wonderful life, but it is not for everyone.

For exact costs of everything from housing to foodstuffs to *huaraches,* I cannot recommend a better investment than a subscription to *Mexico Living & Travel Update,* published by MRTA and written by Jean and John Bryant. Subscriptions are $25 a year. John and Jean are typical of the type of people who fit in so well in Mexico. They manage to be frugal without being miserable, even though John is a recovering banker.

They live the lifestyle they have chosen and are kind enough to share it with others. They tell it like it is and the writing style is very good. John has also published a book, *Mexico Living and Travel* (it is $29.95 with postage and handling; order it from MRTA, P.O. Box 2190, Ste. 23, Pahrump, NV 89041-2190). It is the very best of the many books out there. He has lived in Mexico for many years. My little book will give you a taste of what it is like to live there. His book is the full-course dinner. If, after reading this, you believe living in Mexico may be for you, then order his book. It will be money well spent. It is geared more to the retiree than to the businessman or the bohemian.

Housing in General

Thanks to the many foreigners who shared the following information with me and to Bob and Hazel Acosta, San Xavier Insurance agents in Tucson, Arizona. I have included some exact figures with the following caveats: nothing in Mexico is exact or remains the same. Still, they will give you an idea of what housing costs can run.

Finding a Place to Live

> Don't expect to arrange a place to live before you leave home.

First of all, don't think that you will be able to take care of this before you leave the United States. I have known a few people who have done this, either because they had friends or saw ads in the gringo newspapers from the places where they wanted to go. Some of them got good deals, but they cheated themselves out of one of the greatest experiences of living in a foreign land.

After you settle in, you will find that all your new expatriate buddies will have tales to tell of how they found their perfect habitat. As a newcomer, you will eat these stories up. Just to get you started, I will tell you how I ended up in my home in Pto. Escondido, Oaxaca.

A PERSONAL STORY

I didn't intend to end up in Oaxaca. When I left New Orleans, feeling about as down in the dumps as a man could who had just lost his girlfriend, his father and his fortune, I didn't know where I wanted to go. All I knew was that life had given me a wonderful opportunity to start over because it had taken away everything I had. I knew I wanted to write a book and didn't want to work in the real world while I did it. I went to a friend's near

Mobile, Alabama, and lived for free in his boathouse for a few weeks. I very nearly rented a place on the beach in Alabama for $300 a month, because I was afraid to take the leap and move to Mexico. I had fallen prey to the negative stories about Mexico! After all, the weather in Alabama was almost warm enough for me and it would have been less hassle. Had I done that, I would have cheated myself out of a wonderful experience.

I finally **followed my heart and not my head** and headed south. A friend told me about a paradise—Tuxpan, Veracruz. I left with high hopes. Tuxpan is a nice enough place, but the beach was gray and it gets some cold weather. I moved on.

After checking out several other places, I found myself on a bus going to Acapulco one night. At least I thought it was going to Acapulco. My Spanish was pretty poor and I didn't realize that it wasn't going in the **direction** of Acapulco. It stopped for the night in Pto. Escondido, Oaxaca. Something came over me when I saw the lights ringing the horseshoe bay. I fell in love. I knew this was to be my home.

> *Don't let a few failures depress you. When one door shuts, a better one opens. Have faith.*

Everywhere I asked for a place to live. The local medico who owned a pharmacy and spoke English said he had just the place for me. It was nice, all right. It looked rather like the place in Dothan, Alabama. It also cost more. I told him it was too expensive, so he showed me his second set of monopoly houses. These were thatched-roof huts with one room and a dirt floor.

He magnanimously offered one to me for a mere $250 a month. I was really sad. He was disgusted with me and informed me that if I couldn't afford that price, I would never find anything. Chances are you will run into the same type of landlord. Ignore him. He was just trying to sell me what he had and charge me what he thought the market would bear. If he didn't rent to me, there would be some other sucker tomorrow.

Discouraged, I thought I would have to abandon my dream of living in Mexico and writing my great book. I was on the beach, taking one last sunbath, when a small kid approached me. He made me understand that he knew of a house for rent. I followed him over the road, across the bridge, down a ravine, across a stream and up a dirt hill. At the sleeping pig we turned left. Great, I thought, this has got to be a dump.

It wasn't. It was a comfortable, large, one-room concrete house with a concrete floor and my own bathroom. It even had a sink and a two-burner propane stove! It overlooked the bay and had a hammock on my front porch where I could watch the sunset. Man, it was heaven. The rent was $90 a month. Because the owner wanted to be paid in pesos, and the peso was devaluing at about 20% a year, my rent could only go down. I took it.

I stayed there for the better part of a year. I wrote my book and then, one day, it was just time to leave. I'd fallen in love with a woman instead of a place and she was back in the States.

The moral of this story is twofold. Don't set your hopes on a town until you have seen it, and don't get discouraged if you don't find what you want and can afford right away. It pays to shop and to be patient.

Renting

If you are in a gringo town and want to be in the "community," then you can expect to pay **$600–$2,000 a month,** depending on your tastes and luck. If you want to live on the ocean, count on paying a minimum of $1,200 a month. If you want to live in Baja, you can figure that it will cost you about 40% more to live. In Cabo San Lucas, for instance, it costs about as much to live as in southern California. These prices are for two-bedroom condos and some two-bedroom houses away from the beach areas.

If you want to live in a gringo town, but get away from *gringolandia,* then you can figure on spending $300–$800 a month. This is for a one- or two-bedroom apartment or a small house in a Mexican community. It will be perfectly safe and your neighbors will be middle-class Mexicans. If you rent a room from a family, you can expect to pay $100–$200, depending on your negotiating skills and luck. At this price, meals will not be included, but they shouldn't be exorbitant, if you want them. As I said earlier, if you choose a small town with few other foreigners, you can find abodes for $100–$150 a month.

Finding a rental in Mexico is not like finding one in the United States. You ask. You ask everyone you meet, from the bellboy to the gas station attendant to the hotel manager. You ask other expats. There are those who are living cheaply and those who are living large. Take the advice of either, as you prefer. If you are a member of AA, you will have a built-in network of friends.

Look for signs in the windows of houses you would like to rent. **The sign may not be for that house,** but it will lead you to someone who has a house to rent. Go ahead and check out the local newspapers; it can't hurt. In gringo towns, you will find notices put up where gringos congregate: restaurants, laundries, RV parks. I got my place in Pto. Escondido because one of the owner's sons came up to me on the beach.

RV Living

There are lots of full-timers living in Mexico, mainly during the winter months. Now you can leave a trailer in Mexico and go home, technically that is. I don't know anyone who has done it. Like most changes in Mexico, I will believe it when I see it. Regard-

Smart RVers flock south like Canada geese in the winter.

less, there are several thousand RVers who spend six months a year there.

There are many RV parks. They vary a lot in quality and price. Some are quite nice, with concrete pads, storage sheds, club rooms, activities, Jacuzzis and electric, water and sewer hookups. **Some are primitive,** merely a place to park. Most are somewhere in between. The upscale ones will cost about $300–$500 a month. The midrange ones will run about $200–$300 a month. The basic ones are about $100–$150 a month. In the Baja, there are several basic places with no facilities for about $75 a month. You can also park on a beach there for nothing. I don't recommend this in other parts of Mexico, but the Baja is a different case.

The electrical current is variable, with surges and dips, so it is a good idea to protect yourself from that. Also, you will need a very long extension cord, 100 feet ought to do it, although 150 feet couldn't hurt. **The electrical outlets are not necessarily polarized** and sometimes they are hooked up backwards, so bring a voltage tester and an inexpensive adapter (sold in U.S. and Mexican hardware stores) that will convert your three-prong plug to a two-pronger.

In the Pacific Coast towns like Kino Bay, San Carlos, Guaymas, Mazatlán, Pto. Vallarta, Melaque/San Patricio and Manzanillo, the popular parks tend to fill up during the winter, but there are always spaces at some of the less popular ones.

In the Baja, the parks between Tijuana and Ensenada are often full of permanents, year-round. In Bahia Los Angeles, Mulegé, La Paz and Los Cabos, there will be plenty of room, though some parks can be full during the winter. Prices are high.

On the **Gulf Coast, there is always room and the prices tend to be lower.** There are not as many parks, but there are enough to make a trip there enjoyable. Try the **Emerald Coast** between Tecolutla and Veracruz.

In the Yucatan, there are plenty of parks on the beach. Prices tend to be similar to Baja parks.

Be sure your tires are in good shape, as the roads can be rough on them, and half-size tires are rare in Mexico. **Invest in a set of heavy-duty springs. Don't overload your rig.** You are going to do more bouncing than you would in the United States. There are many toll roads in Mexico, but some are bouncy. For a complete guide to RV parks, order the *Traveler's Guide to Mexican Camping* from a bookstore or my web page. Some books will tell you that there is a special toll rate for RVs. Forget it. That was one of those ideas that lasted for a few weeks and then was forgotten about. Tolls are high, and based on the number of wheels you have—except in Sonora. A representative toll (very much subject to change) is about $150 to drive from Nogales, Arizona, to Mazatlán, Sin. You can take the free roads, but the wear and tear on your vehicle and the aggravation, particularly if you are a first-timer, will make you wish you had spent the bucks. If you break down, don't worry. Mexican mechanics are among Mexico's hidden treasures. They can fabricate parts if they don't have them—in most cases.

The **Green Angels** will probably find you and help you. They are mechanics who work for the tourism department. They patrol the highways looking for people who need assistance. Their help is free, but a tip is appreciated.

Buying a House

BEWARE of buying on a "contract of usage," or on land that used to be an *ejido.* Several gringos in Ensenada may lose their homes because of this. Because of errors in the original *ejido* grant, the original owners were able to reclaim the land, threatening to evict those who had built beautiful homes there. This dispute was part of the public record dating back to 1949, so do adequate research before buying or leasing land anywhere in

Mexico. By early 2000, the U.S. and Mexico federal governments were still involved in trying to work out a fair settlement. It will be resolved soon. While there is nothing wrong with a "contract of usage" deal, just be sure you know what you are getting into. Check my newsletter and website for the results. *Stick with property that has a clear title or can be put into a bank trust.*

There are currently some real bargains for house buyers. Many sellers have cut their asking prices by 30–40%.

Decent houses in small towns can be had for $25,000–$40,000. In cities, the range is $50,000–$90,000. In a gringo community, with golf and gated communities, expect to pay at least $150,000 for a three-bedroom house with a yard. This could easily double or triple for a luxurious home.

Financing—There are now some financial institutions that will finance a home purchase for 70% of the appraised value. They charge 2–3% over the prevailing U.S. rates. The term will be for fifteen years. Some charge an origination fee of 1.5% or a flat $250. Your real estate broker can fill you in on the details needed to get this financing. Realtors in the Baja and San Carlos, Sonora, have offered this for the past few years.

If you want to live on the ocean, a condo will run from $60,000 to $200,000 and up. If you want to buy something in a predominately Mexican subdivision, you can cut your costs by about one-third. A two-bedroom house can cost as little as $40,000 (but you will really have to look to find one). Typical prices are in the $60,000–$80,000 range. In a small town, you can find places for much less, but they will require a lot of looking.

Before you consider buying anything, **please buy two books:** Ginger Combs–Ramirez's *The Gringo's Investment Guide* (Monmex Publishing, P.O. Box 1158, Ennis, MT 59729; 1-800-883-2712), and Dennis John Peyton's *How to Buy Real Estate in Mexico* (2220 Otay Lakes Road, Ste. 502, East Lake, CA 91915; 1-800-LAW-MEXICO; website: www.lawmexico.com).

Both books are good and they each give you a different perspective on buying property. Both can tell you what you need to know. Both authors have lived in Mexico and own property there. Ginger's book is the more readable of the two. Dennis is a lawyer (approved to practice in both Mexico and the United States) and his writing style is more lawyerlike. He covers details that you might never think of.

42

I am not going to go into the step-by-step details of purchasing property like they do, but here is a general guide. The most important thing to remember is: **buyer beware.** Mexico is a different country with different laws. There are some very good, honest realtors in Mexico and many of them are members of A.M.P.I. The **real estate industry** in Mexico is **not as highly regulated** as in the United States. The members of this association are generally regarded as subscribing to higher ethical standards than non-members. Still, this is no guarantee that there are not some unscrupulous ones in the bunch. Also, just because a realtor is a member of Century 21 or some other name you are familiar with *(I am not singling them out),* that doesn't mean that they subscribe to the high standards of the parent organization in the United States. The Mexican realty has bought a franchise, and in your contract it will state that you cannot sue the parent organization if something goes awry.

The best way to protect yourself is to ask for references. Then check them out. Also, ask several other foreign property owners whom they deal with and what their opinion is. People are always happy to give their opinion of other people. Then trust your own judgment. Some gringos assume that because a realtor speaks English he is honest. I have never found that language skills had anything to do with integrity.

You can buy property from another gringo or Mexican and bypass the realtor. Again, don't assume that the other party is angelic. He could also, in good faith, be selling you something that he doesn't completely own.

Once you have decided that a realtor is working in your best interest, don't be in a hurry. That is considered bad form by Mexicans. Sellers who know you are a gringo and see you are in a hurry expect to get top dollar. Wait a while and see if the price doesn't come down.

The restricted zone and fideicomisos.

If you are buying property in mainland Mexico, away from the *restricted zone,* you can get a title. If you are in the restricted zone, then the title will be held for you in a trust by a bank. The restricted zone is any land within 50 kilometers (32 miles) of the coast or 100 kilometers (64 miles) from the border. In these areas, you will be given a *fideicomiso,* or real estate trust. A Mexican bank is set up as the trustee and holds the title for you. The bank is the owner of the property but you are entitled to enjoy the rights of ownership as if you owned the property. You can sell or will the property to whomever you wish at its fair market value for a period of fifty years. The trust is renewable.

Some people have a fear of this. Yes, there is a danger that the banks could be nationalized and all foreign investments could be declared null, but this is incredibly unlikely. There is that risk in any foreign country, but it is so small that I wouldn't worry about it.

Because the trend today is for the globalization of Mexico and the privatization of banks and other formerly government-owned businesses, I don't foresee this happening. If it did happen, it wouldn't make any difference if a bank held your deed or you had it under your mattress. In fact, I think that you are better off in this unlikely scenario if you have a bank to go to bat for you.

Ginger pointed out to me that there is another advantage of a bank holding the deed. If you are an absentee owner and will be gone for long periods of time, there is the possibility (like in this country) that squatters could take over your house and land. If they know that the bank is the owner, they are not likely to try this. If they did, the bank would take care of evicting them.

However, a Mexican friend of mine scoffed at this advice. He doesn't think the bank cares about anything except collecting their money. This is typical of Mexico. You ask two people and you get two different answers. Ginger was speaking from personal experience and so was he. Who's right? I tend to side with my Mexican friend. The best thing to do is ask other expats what their experience has been—and then trust your own instincts.

There is a fee for setting up the *fideicomiso,* dependent on the value of your property. A rough guide is that it might cost $2,000–$3,000 or more. Then there will be annual administrative fees, which are insignificant, perhaps a couple hundred dollars a year. Mexican banks used to have a reputation for being inhospitable and bureaucratic. They deserved it. This

Notario publico—it doesn't mean what you think.

is changing and they are becoming more competitive and more customer service-oriented. **Shop around.** Find one you like. They are still sometimes a pain to deal with, but they are a lot better than they used to be.

Okay, now that you've found your dream home, the fun begins. **You don't need an attorney as well as a notary public.** The notary can do all the paperwork for you. Patience is a virtue here, as you have entered the bureaucratic zone, not unlike the twilight zone.

A *notario publico,* or notary public, is a licensed attorney who is also a de facto representative of the government. He will have something called a *cédula profesional.* This is his professional license and has his picture on it. Although he does not represent the government, he is responsible for seeing that real estate transactions are legal. He is responsible for making sure that all legal niceties are taken care of, that the seller has clear title to the land, that it is not part of an *ejido* or public land grant (this system is being dismantled as we speak, but there is still a chance that old land claims could conflict with your purchase) and that all taxes are paid. As you can see, there is no correlation between the "notary" title in Mexico and the same title in the United States.

All of these things are going to take time. You will have to deal with a host of Mexican officials in preparing your paperwork. **Do not be in a hurry and do not be arrogant.** Treat each of the people you meet with the utmost respect. Do not belittle the people involved in the seemingly endless bureaucracy that you have to deal with. These people have a job to do and they will do it their way in their time. If you get angry or show your frustration, you will only slow the process down. Patience is not just a virtue in Mexico—it is a necessity.

Condominium ownership will be a little more streamlined, because there is often an American-based company at the back of the deal. You will still have to provide various documents and go through many of the same procedures—or you should. Just because someone is selling you a condo doesn't mean he has clear title. It always pays to have a *notario publico* check out any deal you get involved with.

An Overview of Costs—Central America

Most of what I said about Mexico applies to Guatemala and Costa Rica too, with one major caveat. Depending on the fluctuation of the quetzal against the dollar, Guatemala can be considerably cheaper than Mexico. At the moment, it is not, but who's to say that will be true in a year or so?

A few years ago, you could get by in Guatemala for one-half of what you'd spend in Mexico. Today, the peso is weaker against the dollar than the quetzal, and, in general, Guatemala is more expensive than it used to be.

An expatriate who has settled in can still live more cheaply in Guatemala. Even so, today it is possible to live more basically in Guatemala and consequently more cheaply. The Indians certainly do it. Mexico is a rich country by comparison.

Central America is a mixed bag, but generally cheaper. It is for more adventurous souls, though.

I know people who rent very small houses for $100 a month, but they are away from tourist areas and in a Guatemalan community. Generally, in **Panajachel or Antigua, you can expect to pay about 70–80%** of what you would pay for the same type of home in Mexico. You can also pay twice what you would in Mexico. There are some very nice places for rent in each of those towns. If you are unfortunate enough to have been transferred to Guatemala City (otherwise, why would anyone live there?), you will probably spend more on housing than you would in the United States, but less than in Mexico City.

Food in Guatemala may be a little cheaper, and transportation is cheaper. You can also live in decent basic hotel rooms that cater to foreigners for $7–$10 a day. You will find them after talking to several expats in the area. You will also probably have a wait to get into one. As in Mexico, you could rent a room from a family and save a bundle—if that sort of lifestyle is for you.

Other things will be considerably cheaper. Maids will cost half of what they do in Mexico. Some foodstuffs will be cheaper, and some will be more expensive. Imported goods will cost more than in Mexico. Electricity will run about the same—close to stateside prices—but you will use less. There's no need for air-conditioning, and some people even get by without heat. Others have to have a space heater to take the edge off, but only late at night and early in the mornings. During the days everything warms up. Eating out can be cheaper, but only if you stick to the basics.

Costa Rica is expensive in comparison to the other two countries. The standard of living is also quite a bit higher. A good rule of thumb is to figure that it will cost you about 30–50% more to live a comparable lifestyle in Costa Rica than in Mexico. San Jose is very expensive in terms of rentals. The "secure" places will cost you an arm and a leg and they will be nothing to brag about. The farther you get away from the city, the better prices get.

Costa Rica has less poverty than Mexico or Guatemala, **more people speak English and there is a better health care system.** There are also

Costa Rica is the most expensive country in Central America.

more Americans per square foot (or so it seems). Consequently, rental prices are higher and more on the levels of the United States. Buying real estate is easier, and the prices are similar to U.S. prices. That doesn't mean California or New York or Chicago prices. It means in comparison to the heartland of the country. Bargains are few and far between in Costa Rica. Yes, one can make money from land speculation, but one can also lose money. Know what you are doing.

Now, **here is a caveat.** Once you get out of San Jose, prices do tend to drop and it is possible to find a habitat at a reasonable cost. Still, it is not a place for those on a marginal fixed income. There is little available in terms of houses, and you could find something in your price range, but only if you shop around.

It will take you from a few weeks to a few months to find budget accommodations ($300–$400 a month). Meanwhile, you will have to pay rental prices similar to those in the United States. Utilities will be similar in price, perhaps a bit more expensive. Fresh foodstuffs will be comparable, and imported goods will be out of sight. The beef is better.

But there are still some bargains in Costa Rica.

A bohemian could still live in Costa Rica, but rock bottom will not be as close to the bottom. I wouldn't rule it out, because it might be a great experience, but I also wouldn't go there expecting to live on $300 a month. Now you can luck into deals housesitting or living in the back of a restaurant, etc., that would make a liar out of me. More power to you. Go give it a shot.

The attractions (as I see them) of Costa Rica are that it is more European than the other choices in Latin America; the country is more "sanitized" with less poverty; the men and women are more European-looking and easier to approach than in Mexico or Guatemala; the land's natural beauty is softer and appeals to environmental types because it is being protected; it is smaller than the other countries, so it is easier to be in the mountains and the beach on the same day. The main reason so many people are hot on Costa Rica is that it has a better PR firm to promote it.

Changes in Latitudes/ Changes in Attitudes

The lifestyle in Mexico will be slower. People will have time to stop and talk. This also means that nothing will happen when you expect it to. There will be less crime against people.

You will be safer walking the streets. There will be petty crimes and robbery of property if you do not take precautions, such as not leaving anything lying around. There will be times when the Latin way of doing things will make perfect sense and be so much easier than our bureaucratic ways. There will follow times when the incredible bureaucracy in Latin America will make Washington, D.C., seem to be a model of efficiency.

You will feel closer to nature. The flip side of this is that those of you sensitive to noise may find it hard to get a good night's sleep because of the braying donkeys, roosters that crow all night long and barking dogs. You will find yourself investing in a white-noise machine, unless you like sleeping with earplugs.

You will rediscover the simple pleasures of your youth—like sitting on a bench in a city park for an evening. You will find yourself experiencing things that you thought you would never do—and enjoying them. You will gain a new acceptance for peoples' differences and be happy for them. You will wake up one day wishing you had never left the States. You will go to bed many times wondering why it took you so long to leave. You will probably find yourself making friends with a wider variety of people from all walks of life than you would have back home. **You will find yourself developing nonlinear thinking, as nothing, absolutely nothing, works consistently the same way twice.** After a short time, you will find yourself saying "Hi" to dozens of people even on a short walk through town.

A little while longer, and you will find yourself involved in the local intrigues of who's sleeping with whom, who got drunk last night and caused a scene. The flip side of that is that your neighbors will help you whenever you have a small problem. It's like living in a small town a couple of decades ago when everyone really did know one another.

Frank Talk About Sex

Condoms are sold openly in *farmacias,* or pharmacies, as well as in supermarkets and department stores like Gigante and Wal-Mart. They are out in the open and in various departments and sometimes right by the register. In Spanish they are called *condoms* (pro-

> *In gringo communities, couples don't break up— they just change partners.*

nounced kon-**domes**). Some American brands like Trojans are available, but specialty brands, like Kimonos, are not. Mexican brands have a bad reputation. Whether it is unfounded or not, I cannot say for sure, but why take a chance, just to save a few pesos. If you have a favorite brand back home, bring a good supply. Although there is probably a limit to the number you are supposed to bring with you, I doubt it would ever be enforced.

Even if you do not use condoms back home, I strongly recommend their use here. For one thing, there are more Mexican homosexuals than you would imagine. Yes, I know that AIDS is not just a homosexual disease, but statistically they are a high-risk group.

How does this affect you, you ask? Well, many Mexican males do not consider themselves homosexuals just because they have had sex with another man. It is only a matter of convenience and not a lifestyle choice. Consequently, it is common for a man to have a quickie with another man, then go home to his wife or girlfriend and have sex.

Although this attitude is changing, it is still common enough for concern. Condom use is still looked down upon and not as popular as it is at stateside. Even if you stick to foreign men or women *(and who says they are any more protected from HIV?),* the community is small enough that you might as well be sleeping with every other sexually active gringo in town. There is a saying among many expats that you don't break up, you merely change partners. Many of them have also been with Latin lovers.

Candid Advice for Women

Some women who live in Latin America shed years and become younger in their attitudes. They find the challenge of living and adapting invigorating. Others, however, age quickly. I have seen this with both sexes, but more so with women.

There are many women who have settlements from divorces or the sales of their houses who flock south to live. **Most of them have a wonderful time and find a new life that is much happier and fuller** than the one they left behind. Many of them

> *Divorce could be the beginning of a new life. When God gives you lemons, you can either pucker up and frown or make lemonade and smile. Many women find a new life, a better life in Mexico than the one they left behind.*

who had spent years in unhappy relationships find themselves and experience a joyful life for the first time. Unfortunately, there are two other scenarios that can be played out. Both can happen to men, with a few slight changes in story line.

The first seems rather inexplicable on the surface. After a few years of living as expatriates, some women become negative and bitter. Perhaps it is a reaction to the fatalism of the Latinos around them, or frustration at the difficulty of getting things done. Maybe it stems from the double standards found in such a male-dominated society. These women become cynical and concentrate on the negatives in life around them.

I have seen young women become old crones in only a few years. To avoid this, I strongly recommend a few visits stateside each year and the honest opinion of a trusted friend to let you know when you start crossing the line. A strong competitive nature when you didn't have one to start with is a bad sign, as is a need to be right all the time over unimportant issues. I don't know the cure, but if you find yourself seeing only the bad, ordering waiters and other help around imperiously and bragging about events in the past that gave you pleasure when everyone else is talking about the present, maybe it is time for you to relocate stateside for a while.

The other scenario involves going into business. This one is far more common and predictable. It happens in the States too. A woman will move

> *Is that gleam in his eyes because he is starstruck or is it a glimmer of greed?*

down, usually in a vulnerable state, and find herself attracted to a Latin man. There is nothing wrong with that. There are some very good Latin men and some marriages that have lasted for many years between *gringas* (or *gueras,* which means blondes, but is used as a synonym for *gringas*) and Latin men. What is wrong, though, is that there is a subculture of Latin males (usually at beach resorts or other areas that attract lots of *gringas*) that preys on these women. These guys are young and very romantic. They sweep lonely *gringas* off their feet, women who would not fall for this at home. After the hook is set, they suggest that there could be a way for the two of them to be so much happier.

How's that, you ask? Simple, if we started a little restaurant (or bought a fishing boat, or a boutique or a hotel, etc.), then I could quit my job as a fisherman (or clerk or bellboy, etc.) and we could spend more time together. Sounds dreamy, you say, the visions of being a foreign business owner dancing in your head. Of course, you have all that money doing nothing back home and this could be a perfect investment. Of course, you would put it in his name to avoid the complications of Mexican laws. Some men would even be willing to marry you, to help you out.

Whoa! You may think I am being silly, that you are smarter than that. Yes, you probably are—under normal circumstances. Unfortunately, these guys are good (a lot smoother than I will ever be, that's for sure), and the romantic Mexican or Guatemalan moon has powers that we don't understand. I have personally known a number of women who fell for these scams. What usually happens is that you do get the business going and one day find yourself spending all your time working, while he is out "promoting" it.

Often he is "promoting" another business with a new *gringa* in town, or maybe just making a new friend. Because I often revisit the same locales, I can tell the stage of the relationship by the atmosphere and quality of such hotels and restaurants. By the time she leaves, disgusted, I have usually taken it out of my books.

Please don't get me wrong, or take this out of context. I also know couples who have run successful businesses and had great marriages. I am all for romance, and it's no skin off my nose whom you date. Just take it easy and take a second look. Ask around among other women and find out if this guy has a reputation for romancing women into business. It will be worth the effort. If a deal is too good to be true and must be closed today, get suspicious. Just take your time and I wish you every happiness in the world. If you choose to get married, be sure that you understand what the Latin culture is. Even if your husband-to-be is one of the most liberated men on the face of the planet, be ready to marry his family. This is both a blessing and a curse. See my description of that below. Test the waters before you dive headfirst.

51

One last thing. I'm not your papa and have no real stake in this issue, but a number of my women friends have asked me to include a paragraph about the following. There is yet another type of fellow who can turn out to be bad news. He is the older guy who hangs around with the "student" group. He will be a romantic sweet-talker and being with him will be great fun. Have fun, enjoy yourself, but don't expect it to come to more than that.

These guys are not looking for a lasting relationship. Why else do you think they are hanging around with twenty-year-olds? Accept them for what they are and don't get too involved. If they want to come to visit you in your home country, fine, but don't be surprised if they are also visiting a number of other women. Some of them would like to marry a *gringa* in order to get their papers to live in the United States.

Candid Advice for Men

Just between us guys, let's be honest. **The reason a lot of you want to live in Latin America is so that you can meet and marry a *Latina*.** There's nothing wrong with that. There are some *Latinas* who would love to marry a gringo, some for true love and some

Okay, guys, maybe you'd better read this. Things are different for you too.

because we have reputations as good providers (if not as lovers). First of all, remember that **not all *Latinas* are interested in you.** Many of them are very happy with their own culture and men and don't want some **ignorant, uncultured gringo** coming along and bothering them.

Although these women may wear tight skirts and stockings, that doesn't mean they are loose. Many of them get their fashion sense from warped TV ads and are nice Catholic girls underneath, so use some class or you will risk offending her brothers. They all have brothers, none of whom has a sense of humor about his sister. If you find a woman you like and begin to court her, it will probably take longer than you think, at least in Mexico and Guatemala. Costa Rica is more westernized.

You will be marrying a Latin family. That means that you had better like children, grandchildren and in-laws, because you will have plenty of each. Your wife-to-be will always defer to your mother-in-law-to-be. Get used to it. The extended family provides a warm, loving group to help you when you need it. It can ease your entry into social and business circles. It can also mean a meddlesome set of in-laws and a lot less alone time. Some love it. Some don't. Test the waters before you go swimming. Men aren't expected to share the parenting fifty-fifty. You won't have to do as much with the children as you would be expected to in a stateside marriage. You will, however, be expected to provide the necessities damn well. If the two of you start a business, you may find that if you don't do a very good job she will run it better than you. A lot of guys told me they moved to Latin America for the adventure and found themselves years later living a far more bourgeois life as shopkeepers and Babbitts than they would have back home. Think about it. Then all the best to you.

If you are younger, you may simply be interested in dating—whether *Latinas* or *gringas,* it doesn't matter. You will find it easier, in general, to date *gringas,* but maybe not as easy as you think. First of all, there are many who are traveling with other women because they don't want to be bothered by guys. There are also a number of them who are only interested in dating Latin men. Then there are those who have "gone native" and will refuse to speak English. Rather than waste your time bothering them, move on to greener pastures.

Many women will be receptive to traveling together and after that, you will simply have to work your charms. You will find European women to be more interesting than American women and easier to get to know. The Europeans tend to hang around ruins and take more budget accommodations. They, of course, like the beaches, and are particularly attracted to the topless beaches. Your chances will be better if you speak some Spanish and at least appear as if you know what is going on. It can't hurt to learn a few French, German or Italian phrases.

You will meet Germans and French everywhere, and the Italians tend to congregate on beaches, particularly the Pacific Coast below Acapulco and the Yucatan. Be prepared to meet a lot of *Quebecois,* or French-speaking Canadians from Quebec. They tend to keep to their own little groups, so you are probably better advised to not have great expectations about breaking into their cliques. Many of them are wonderful people, once you get to know them. Of course, if you speak French, they are more likely to think you are wonderful too.

After you have been living in a place for a while, there is a tendency to become arrogant and condescending to newcomers and tourists. Believe me, this does nothing but keep otherwise interesting people from getting to know you. Friendliness and helpfulness will get you where you want to be.

Candid Advice for Gays and Lesbians

You will find Mexico a giant contradiction. While the strong Catholic background and macho culture are disapproving of your lifestyles, you will also find a general "live-and-let-live" attitude. Some areas are, of course, more gay-friendly than others and I tell you where they are. In general, as long as you are not too outrageous, you will get along with the Mexicans. If you act like you are in New York or Los Angeles, you will find life more difficult. There are fewer hate crimes in Mexico, so you will be much safer than you would be in the States. There is

The straight scoop for alternative lifestyles.

one exception. Those who take up with young Mexican boys are treated not only with scorn, but they are often physically attacked by the local citizenry and beaten by the constabulary. In jail, they are beaten regularly. Even if the worst does not happen, and you fall in love with a young man, be careful. A few men told me about coming home and finding everything they owned gone. There was nothing they could do. Going to the police would have only put them at more risk. They chalked it up to a life lesson. Learn from them.

Lesbians have it better and worse than gay men. It is common for Latin women to be more affectionate in public than in the States, so gay women displaying affection will not be considered unusual. What drives some of them up the wall is the typical Latin *machismo,* which makes American males seem positively liberated. My lesbian friends have told me that those women who are happiest in Latin America simply have learned to accept the attitudes and attention that come with *machismo.* Those who are the unhappiest are the ones who try to change the Latin men. Live and let live and enjoy your life.

Life in Latin America can be a mostly freeing experience, although occasionally confining. There are more *Latinos* who are gay than you would suspect, and there are clubs in all the major cities. Just remember to act as straight as you can when you are dealing with the police. They are often really homophobic.

There is a book, *A Man's Guide to Mexico* (Centurion Press), that is a veritable cornucopia of information specific to gay men, including a run-down on the nightlife.

Where to Live—Mexico

Mexico is a huge and diverse country. It encompasses climates as varied as deserts to tropical jungle to mile-high mountains and areas with springlike weather all year long. If you are being transferred by your company, they probably did not pick a spot based on the lovely climate. But you could still get lucky. If you have more control

> God made both heaven and hell. Man usually manages to make his own without any help from a Higher Power.

over your destiny, then you will have to choose an area that appeals to you. Visit several and stay for a few months in each before making up your mind.

The following thumbnail sketches are meant to give you an overview. You can only get to know a place by going there and hanging out for a while. Even if you buy one of those books that goes on for pages and pages on life in any one of these locales, you won't really know if it is for you until you get there. What I have tried to do is to give you an idea of what the towns are really like, without the hype and hyperbole, from someone who has spent enough time in each and has talked to enough locals to eliminate the chaff. My opinions are just opinions.

There will be some who will disagree with me, particularly boosters of some of the towns I am not particularly high on. I call them as I see them and have tried to be impartial. Your heaven may be my hell. I have simply tried to state that some places may not be your cup of tea if you are cut from a different cloth. Why beat your head against a wall trying to fit into a community because all the other books say it is a "wonderful place to retire"?

Why not try to find a place where the unique you will be happy? *That's what life is about—being happy.* We've all spent too much of our lives trying to fit into somebody else's mold. Now that you are moving away, go somewhere where you can be yourself.

When I took off to find a place to live in Mexico, I had advice from dozens of people about where I should go. I was so mixed up that I thought they knew more than I did about what was good for me, so I tried to like a few places that obviously were wrong for me. I investigated about a dozen towns before I found the one I settled in—and even then I didn't make the perfect choice. Had I had a book like this, I would have at least tried out a few others.

Guadalajara & Environs

◎ *Guadalajara, Jalisco*

Altitude:	5,092 ft.
Population:	3,000,000 and growing
Climate:	Perfect year-round, though some think it's a little hot in the summer.
Housing:	Many choices from moderate to expensive.
Ambiente:	Cultured, sophisticated, big-city. A good number of foreigners.
Medical care:	Excellent.
Area code:	3

PROS

This is the place most people think of when they think of retiring to Mexico. The climate is practically perfect, a perpetual spring. The city offers cultural attractions from symphonies to plays to museums to picturesque markets. Public transportation is excellent. There are enough activities by the foreign community so that you will not feel alone.

Medical care is top-notch and there is a wide variety of hospitals and doctors to choose from. Because it is a city, you can buy a wide variety of products from food to furniture, from all over Mexico, at reasonable prices. It has several fine golf courses and country clubs. There are some RV parks here that have a real sense of community, and many of the residents have returned here year after year. It is easy to drive to, either from the Arizona border or the Texas border.

The cuisine here is truly international, with many different countries represented. You can spend as much or as little as you want when eating out.

There is an English-language newspaper. There are some **English AA and Alanon** groups here, but they are not as active as in Chapala. There are fewer members and fewer meetings. There are hot springs a few hours away. The American consul is at Progreso #175 CP, phone: (3) 625-2998, fax: (3) 626-6549. Duty Officer and after-hours calls: (3) 626-5553. Office hours: 8 A.M.–4:30 P.M. Mailing address: APDO Postal #39-10, 44171 Guadalajara, Jal.

58

The Canadian consul is located at: The Consulate of Canada, Hotel Fiesta Americana, Local 31, Aurelio Aceves 225, Col. Vallarta Pte., 44100 Guadalajara, Jal., phone: (011-52-3) 616-5642, 615-6270, 615-62, 615-6266, fax: (011-52-3) 615-8665. Consul and Trade Commissioner: Ms. J. Dauberry. Territory includes the state of Jalisco except Pto. Vallarta, Chapala Lake region and Jalisco Coast.

The **American Legion** Post #3 is at San Antonio #143, Col. Las Fuentes 4, Guadalajara, Jal., APDO Postal #31-401. Adjutant: Royce Wheeler.

There is a **synagogue** at Juan Palomar y Amaas #651, Fracc. Monraz, 44670 Guadalajara, Jal., phone: (3) 641-6779, 641-6463. They also have kosher products from Technologia Narciso, Monterrey, and import delicatessen foods from Mexico City.

Language Schools

There are several language schools here. The Mexican–North American Cultural Institute of Jalisco is a wonderful place that can help you in learning Spanish and about the culture of the area. Their address is: Enrique Diáz de León #300, Guadalajara, Jal., phone: (3) 625-5838, 625-4101. You can take classes at the university. The Instituto Cultural, Enrique Diáz de León (Tolsa), 300, 44170 Guadalajara, Jal., phone: (3) 825-4101, 825-5838, is a member of the Assn. of U.S.–Mexican Binational Centers and is a good one.

CONS

This is a huge city with a population of between three and five million. It now has pollution problems, though nothing as severe as Mexico City, but as bad as many big cities in the United States. Driving is challenging, to say the least. Even I am challenged there. **Traffic jams and rush-hour traffic are facts of life.** The cost of living is reasonable, but if you want to rent or buy a house in the foreign community, the cost will be high. Outside these gringo enclaves, prices are only a little bit higher than they would be in a smaller city. The idea of living in a big city just because the weather is nice just doesn't appeal to me. Unless I had a business or artistic reason to be here, I would move instead to the Lake Chapala area.

IN-BETWEENS

There is a diverse group of foreigners living here. There are embassy personnel from around the world and executives and employees of international corporations. Because it is a business city, it is easier to get things done here than in a smaller town or a "retirement" community. *The Wall Street Journal* and *The New York Times* are available.

There are stockbrokers, FedEx, DHL, generally good telephone and fax service and the opportunity to dress up for events. It is an excellent place to conduct business as there are convention centers, and the major hotels can put your clients up in the style they are used to anywhere in the world; they know how to cater to the business traveler. There is an international airport with direct flights to the United States and good connections to the rest of the world. It is a very sophisticated city.

The Mexican businesspeople who live here speak English quite well. The foreign businesspeople here have mostly learned to speak Spanish out of respect for their Mexican colleagues. The foreign retirees are a mixed lot. Some of them have chosen to integrate themselves into the community and speak Spanish. Because it is possible to live here and never speak a lick of Spanish, many of the old-timers have chosen that option. Some have told me that the retirees living here tend to be on more of a budget than those in the lakeside communities.

If you are a younger person thinking of living here, you will not have much (foreign) company for socializing with, except for those working for foreign corporations. If you want to **study Spanish or art,** it is a fine place. If you want to live the life of an artist, and would like to meet Mexican artists, my vote would be to hang out here a couple of months to absorb the culture and then move on.

❂ *Chapala and Ajijic, Jalisco*

Altitude:	4,922 ft.
Population:	50,000

Continued on next page

Climate:	A little cooler than Guadalajara. Perfect. Rainy season: June–Sept.
Housing:	Available, but tends to be pricey. With the population surging in winter with "snowbirds," the inexpensive places are gone quickly.
Ambiente:	An American-Canadian colony.
Medical care:	Very good, and Guadalajara is only 26 miles away.
Area code:	376

PROS

Although I lump these two together, **they are distinctly different** places. Ajijic is a little more upscale and has a different sense of community than Chapala, though these distinctions will only be apparent after spending some time in the area. For the purposes of this book, we can consider them one and not be too out of line. These medium-sized towns are about an hour away from Guadalajara, yet worlds apart.

These are the places most prospective retirees mean when they say "Guadalajara." They've been promoted as retirement communities for decades and have quite an active collection of gringos living in them. There are so many American and Canadian organizations that you could spend all of your time involved in them.

The Lake Chapala Society, 16 de Septiembre #16-A, is quite a deal. They have an English-language lending library, social events, charity projects, a talking book library, a videotape library and more. They also publish a nifty directory of their members. You should join them while you are here.

While bridge and other social pursuits are the norms, there are also charitable causes to get involved in. These groups will help local schools, clinics or other community projects. You will never feel alone here, and many people feel that it offers many of the conveniences of a retirement community in the United States.

Medical care is adequate for most situations, but for major surgery or emergencies, you will have to go to Guadalajara. There is a fine **golf course** and country club. There is an **English-language newspaper**, *The Guadalajara Colony Reporter.* You can subscribe to the paper from the United States if you want to get an idea of what is going on in the area. A six-month subscription costs $50 and a year is $75 (make checks payable to *Colony Reporter*). Their Mexican address is: Duque de Rivas #254, 44140 Guadalajara, Jal., Mexico. Their U.S. address for subscriptions is: 9051-C Siempre Viva Rd. #5452, San Diego, CA 92173.

There is no smog and the lifestyle is relaxed. There is an adequate variety of restaurants, but it is not a gourmet's delight. Food costs are reasonable to high. There is plenty of **English AA** and other 12 Step groups with a large membership. There is an Alano Club. Nearby Jocotepec has a hot spring. The **American Legion** has a strong post here.

Internet

There are good **Internet** connections here and a group that runs a dandy home page, http://mexconnect.com. They can provide you with a tremendous amount of information about living in the area or Mexico in general. ISPs include CompuServe, which offers 5 hours for $18.65, the University of Guadalajara (the fastest connection), which offers 5 hours for $18, and Infosel, which has a deal of 100 hours for $70. They are slower, but you can always get on. America Online is here too, but you have to call Mexico City (long distance) to get on. There is another server, Vianet, which is not recommended. All give you 1 MB of e-mail storage.

CONS

Housing costs are high. Any place with a large foreign population will have higher costs than places where the competition for housing is not so fierce. You are paying for the convenience of having a lot of English spoken and the companionship of your countrymen. You can avoid these costs by living farther away, down the lake. I did meet a woman who pays $300 a month to live in a small hotel.

IN-BETWEENS

It is easy to live here and never interface with the Mexican culture because of all the other foreigners to talk to and the activities of the American Society and other groups. Many of the residents have chosen to isolate themselves this way. Their contact with Mexicans is limited to their maids and shopkeepers.

They often do not travel through the country and know very little outside their area. This is, of course, not a blanket description of all the residents of the area. Many of them came here because they loved Mexico and wanted to live in Mexico. Still there are enough people who are living here only because the weather is great and the costs are lower than for a comparable lifestyle back home to make it worth noting. Most of the foreigners here are retirees in their sixties and beyond. Many of them have been living here, or coming back here, for years and years.

A businessman is unlikely to be transferred here, though if you were willing to commute to Guadalajara, you might find it a pleasant place to live. The drive isn't as bad as the one you might take if you lived in a suburb of Chicago or Houston or Los Angeles or Seattle. If you are younger, you will not find much companionship. If you are an artist or writer, you might possibly want to check it out.

The area attracted D. H. Lawrence and a host of others over the years, and wherever you have wealthy retirees, you have people interested in promoting the arts. The trap I see is that you could get so involved in the society doings that you forget why you came here in the first place. The lifestyle of the foreigners here tends to be **conservative**. Ajijic is a little more upscale, according to local residents. They say that Chapalaites tend to be more on a fixed income and watch their pennies more. Chapala does have more hotels, and the possibility of checking it out for an extended time without making a commitment is greater.

❂ *Jocotepec, Jalisco*

Altitude:	4,922 ft.
Population:	2,000
Climate:	A little cooler than Guadalajara. Perfect. Rainy season: June–Sept.
Housing:	Adequate. Considerably less expensive than Chapala.
Ambiente:	Very Mexican.
Medical care:	Close enough to Chapala so as not to worry.
Area code:	376

PROS

The farther you travel along Lake Chapala, the closer you get to "old" Mexico. Jocotepec (and the other communities along the lake) have a different character, more Mexican in flavor. While it is possible to spend just as much for housing here as in Chapala, **there are also more bargains,** the farther you get away. Of course, you lose some of the amenities in return, but for many that is not a problem. You can stay here and feel a bit more isolated from the social hustle and bustle of Chapala, yet be close enough to drive over and take part in whatever activity pleases you. The physical distance is minuscule, but the "feeling" of distance is enormous. There is a hot spring.

CONS

You have farther to drive for medical care. The distance from the social happenings may be a bother. The accommodations tend to be plainer. Restaurants tend to be Mexican cuisine. There is no golf course.

IN-BETWEENS

Jocotepec and the other communities along Lake Chapala might be more suited to those who want to immerse themselves in Mexico and are willing to learn some Spanish. There are fewer locals who speak English. You could go days here and not speak English unless you wanted to. Artists and writers might find the area more conducive to creating, and the cost of subsistence is less. You will find no foreign businessmen here. A younger person will have no foreign social life, though you could find it somewhat easier to integrate with the locals.

The Heartland— Colonial Mexico

✪ San Miguel de Allende, Guanajuato

Altitude:	5,903 ft.
Population:	40,000
Climate:	Mild winters, rare frost; temperate summers; heavenly in between.
Housing:	One of the priciest places, but there are deals on rentals and house-sitting.
Ambiente:	Cultured, artistic haven. Gringos are very much in evidence.
Medical care:	Adequate.
Area code:	415

PROS

This is a very **pleasant town** in the central highlands (the *Bajio*) of the country. Some people say this is the perfect climate. The weather is brisk most of the year. The summers are rather warm in the day (but not hot) and mildly cool at night. The winters are almost as warm in the day and a little cooler at night.

Here, you will be able to wear a sweater or your leather jacket as often as you like. Even I don't need much more and often only have my leather jacket on because it looks good, not because I am really that chilly.

The town was declared a national historical landmark and it is known for its **colonial architecture**. Because of its landmark statues, no modern-style buildings can be constructed downtown. The narrow, serpentine cobblestone streets that wind through centuries-old stone buildings impart a European feel to the place.

There is a **sizable foreign community** with a number of activities to get involved in. There is an English-language newspaper, *Atención* (Biblioteca Pública de San Miguel, #25 Insurgentes, 37700 San Miguel de Allende, Gto.) and a lending library with English-language books. You should make a contribution to the library if you are in the neighborhood.

An American consular agent, Col. Philip J. Maher, has been around for years and is quite helpful to his countrymen. His address is: Hernandez Macías, #72, phone: (465) 2-2357, fax: (465) 2-1588. He's available Mon., Wed. 9 A.M.–1 P.M. and 4–7 P.M., and Tues., Thurs. 4–7 P.M. There is also an **American Legion Post.** There is a Canadian consulate at the Consulate of Canada, Mesones 38, Interior 15, 37700 San Miguel de Allende, Gto., phone: (011-52-415) 230-25, fax: (011-52-415) 268-56. Honorary Vice Consul: Ms. G. Bisaillion. Territory includes the states of Guanajuato and Querétaro.

There is a **hot spring,** Taboada, with waters of the same mineral content as Baden-Baden, Germany. They are reputed to retard aging. There is a first-class hotel at the springs, Hacienda Taboada. For reservations, call 1-800-321-4622.

Language Schools

One of the most popular reasons for going to San Miguel is to study Spanish at the Instituto Allende, Calle Ancha de San Antonio #20, 37700 San Miguel de Allende, Gto., phone: (465) 2-0190, fax: (465) 2-0190. Others are: Academia Hispano Americana, Mesones 4, phone: (465) 2-0349, fax: (465) 2-2333, and Inter Idiomas, Mesones #15, phone: (465) 2-2177. Some rate the latter two as more demanding than the Instituto.

San Miguel is crawling with artists and writers, some of whom have been known to crawl home after a little too much of the ample nightlife. Robert Mitchum liked the place.

Besides this, there are also many cultural and artistic activities connected to the Instituto. You can take courses in most anything that interests you, either here or at peoples' homes. Writing, photography, painting, sculpting, massage and a wide variety of "touchy-feely" courses or seminars (like

The Course in Miracles, The Celestine Prophesy, Zen, meditation, etc.) are offered all around town. Some of the instructors are quite good in their fields, with international reputations. Some are just sincere. Either way, you will not lack for a group that wants to help you develop your inner or artistic self.

A wide variety of restaurants is available, representing many countries. **Vegetarians** will be well fed here. You can get *The New York Times,* but not daily. Adequate medical treatment is available for minor problems, but for major emergencies you will have to go to Leon or Mexico City. There is a fine golf course and country club. There is an American Legion Post. There is a very active 12 Step community with **AA, Alanon, ACOA and NA,** and probably others are represented. There is an Alano Club.

If you are a single of any age, or lifestyle, you will have many opportunities to meet a partner, either among the foreign community or among the constant stream of travelers—mainly Texans, New Yorkers, Californians and Europeans—though every state in the union is represented. You can find inexpensive hotels and rooms for rent, and, after a while, it is even possible to house-sit for other foreigners. You can also spend a bloody fortune and live in luxury like you have only dreamed of. The choice is yours. There is a good, **honest realtor** I can personally vouch for, Sr. Abraham Cadena, Calle Ancha San Antonio #21, phone: (415) 2-1638, fax: (415) 2-2313. Mailing address: APDO Postal #26, San Miguel de Allende, Gto.

CONS

Real estate here is quite expensive. Although you can rent houses and rooms quite reasonably, you will have to be financially successful to buy something here. If you own a home here, do not go off and leave it empty.

Please do not take what I am about to say out of context. San Miguel is a perfectly safe place to live, but robbery of houses is a real problem. If you do not get a house sitter, you will likely return to find yourself materially liberated. This is probably not true of some of the guarded communities on the outskirts of town, but for most houses in town it is a fact of life.

IN-BETWEENS

San Miguel is more international in flavor than any of the places I will mention. It also has the greatest mix of ages and lifestyles. It is also more liberal than any other place besides Pto. Vallarta. There are more artists and writers and sculptors and photographers per square foot here than anywhere except Santa Fe, New Mexico. There is a local joke that half of the new residents were former directors of the Santa Fe Art Museum. Of course, many of these people are dilettantes, but so what? If you are looking for the "artsy" lifestyle, you will find it here.

You'll meet fellow scribblers or dabblers from all over the world. Once I was looking for a friend of mine and walked into another house. A familiar face asked me if he could help me and I told him whom I was looking for. He politely directed me down the block. It was John Irving. With this diversity of expatriates comes a diversity of lifestyles. **Gays and lesbians** will find it a **gay-friendly** place, with lots of company.

The ages of the foreign residents are all over the place, from the twenties to the nineties. The foreign societies here tend to get involved in local projects and take an interest in the community they live in. The foreign residents tend to speak at least a little Spanish and many of them speak it very well. The foreigners here seem to be genuinely interested in Mexico and are likely to have traveled to other parts of the country. There are few foreign businessmen, though some foreigners own farms in the area.

An excellent resource is *The Insider's Guide to San Miguel* by Archie Dean, a longtime resident. It lists everything from apartments (and costs) and utilities to watch repair. Archie updates it frequently and only does small press runs. Get it in San Miguel or from www.mexicomike.com.

☼ *Guanajuato, Guanajuato*

(No, I didn't mistype it. The name of the city and the state are the same.)

Altitude:	6,471 ft.
Population:	85,000
Climate:	Mild winters, rare frost; temperate summers; heavenly in between.
Housing:	Pricey, but there are deals on rentals and house-sitting.
Ambiente:	Very Spanish, cultured, conservative. Few gringos in residence.
Medical care:	Adequate.
Area code:	415

PROS

"Unique" sums up this small city. Only an hour's drive from San Miguel de Allende, it is another world. It has been called the most European of Mexico's cities. The atmosphere here is more conservative than San Miguel. There is a tremendous amount of **culture** here. Even so, they let me visit occasionally, if I promise not to stay too long.

It is built in a dramatic setting. The houses are built on hills and each one seems to overlook the next. A local joke is that if you want to know what's happening with your neighbors, just lean out your window. Meandering through the middle of the town are a series of subterranean streets that form a mazelike expressway. It's an old mining town and its riches are based mostly on silver. The city center is a car-free zone, which makes life more pleasant and getting around a bit more of a challenge. **If you are not up to walking, then you will find this a very challenging city.**

In the town square *(zócalo)*, there are band concerts at night, a collection of sidewalk cafes and a lot of people to watch. There are often groups that meet in front of the cathedral to begin a *callejonada,* or a singing, drinking stroll through the city's labyrinthine streets. It begins with the troubadours (dressed in period costumes) telling ribald stories on the church steps. After a sufficient crowd has gathered and everyone is properly lubricated from the wine *botas,* they begin serenading and wandering. You shouldn't miss it.

Housing prices here are considerably less than in San Miguel. You can buy or rent a place for about one-third of what you could in San Miguel. Like its sister city, a place in the old section of town will be very romantic and charming and most likely have ancient plumbing. If you choose one of the suburbs, like Marfil, for instance, you will find more spacious and modern quarters.

This was once called the "Beverly Hills" of Guanajuato. It was where the wealthy of the city built their spacious mansions and lovely parks. Then, when silver took a downturn and a series of floods made it less desirable, they abandoned those mansions. Today, the area is again a lovely place to live and has regained some of its bygone grandeur. There are other, more modern developments as well.

There are a lot of cultural and art happenings here, many of which are associated with the university. The crowd is either young or young at heart.

68

Language Schools

There are at least two language schools. The Universidad de Guanajuato, Departamento de Servicios al Estudiante, Lascurain de Retana #5, 36000 Guanajuato, Gto., phone: (473) 2-2770, fax: (473) 2-0278, offers courses and can arrange for you to stay with a family. They also offer for-credit courses and are affiliated with about a dozen universities in the United States.

Another school is the Instituto Falcón, Callejón de la Mora #158, 36000 Guanajuato, Gto., phone: (473) 2-36-94. They are more flexible about the classes and also can arrange for a family stay.

CONS

There is not nearly as much English spoken as in San Miguel. For some this is a plus. On weekends it becomes very crowded, with thousands of *Chilangos* (people from Mexico City) crowding in to escape the smog. It is nearly impossible to find a hotel then and the streets are even more crowded with cars. There is no English AA. The foreign community is small. The close quarters everyone lives in could get to you after a while. The winding and steep streets can be difficult for some people.

IN-BETWEENS

This is a fine choice for someone who wants to get away from other Americans and Canadians. It has a very artistic feel to it, so you probably could write or paint a masterpiece here. The old-world charm gives you a sense of the permanency of place and a feeling of the impermanence of man. It is not for everyone, but it could be an ideal place for someone who is self-sufficient and artistic.

❂ Querétaro, Querétaro

Altitude:	6,024 ft.
Population:	450,000
Climate:	Similar to San Miguel.
Housing:	All price ranges.
Ambiente:	Cultured, big-city, conservative.
Medical care:	Excellent.
Area code:	42

PROS

There is a really good chance that you were transferred here by your American or Canadian company. This is a large city about two hours north of Mexico City on Hwy. 57. It has a pleasant climate and is quite a cultured place.

It is a large manufacturing city and many international plants are located here. The downtown area is old, old, **colonial Mexico,** and one can get a sense of centuries gone by sitting at some of the sidewalk cafes. There are two theaters with international plays, art museums, several golf courses, riding clubs and a polo club. It is cosmopolitan enough to satisfy most and is only a couple of hours (depending on the traffic) from the largest city in the world.

CONS

The foreign community is really small and made up of mostly families of executives and engineers of the aforementioned international plants. The traffic is a pain. Pollution has reared its ugly head. It is a very conservative place and definitely not one where I would choose to live.

IN-BETWEENS

If you want to live in a real Mexican city with the charms of colonial Mexico and the pluses and minuses of a modern city, it would be an okay place to live.

⊙ *Mexico City, or Mexico, D.F.*

Altitude:	7,349 ft.
Population:	21,000,000 and growing
Climate:	Chilly on some winter days, with frost; otherwise temperate. Summers can be warm, but not hot.
Housing:	Expensive and hard to find.
Ambiente:	World-class city. You can find most anything. Sophisticated, business-oriented.
Medical care:	Excellent.
Area code:	5

PROS

I like Mexico City. It is one of the world's greatest cities and is truly international. Although you may not be able to find everything here that you find in New York, you can certainly find a lot more than you would expect. It is a **businessman's town,** with excellent communications, daily copies of *The New York Times, The Wall Street Journal* and the best local newspapers in Mexico and two English-language dailies. The new kid on the block is the *Mexico City Times,* Av. Juarez #100, Col. Juarez, 06040 Mexico, D.F., phone: 518-4262, e-mail: mexcittm@infosel.net.mex. On Saturday, it has the "Guardian" supplement. On Monday, it has *The New York Times* "Week in Review." The older paper is the *Mexico City News,* Balderas #87, Col. Juarez, 06040 Mexico, D.F., phone: 510-9623; www.novedades.com. An electronic paper is *CityView;* www.cityview.com, which covers all the bases for residents, tourists and business travelers. Apart from the usual information— hotels, restaurants, places to see, etc.—it is updated daily with information on museum exhibits, concerts and other current events. It is the most complete of the websites on Mexico City.

With the peso currently trading at about 9.5–10 to the dollar, Mexico City is inexpensive. A friend of mine, Mike Zamba, used to be the editor of the *Mexico City News* and *Mexico Events* magazine and is now an active participant to *The Dallas Morning News* Internet service, **CityView.** In 1993, he paid 3,500 pesos rent for his three-bedroom apartment near the American Embassy. Then, that was about $1,000 a month. He still pays the same rent in pesos, but it is only about $400 with the current peso exchange rate.

The international airport has flights to the United States, Canada, Europe and Asia as well as to Central and South America. Business hotels know how to treat foreign executives. The cuisine is truly international, with many nations represented. **Vegetarians** will have several choices here. There are even **kosher restaurants.** There is more art, culture and history here than you can absorb in two lifetimes. There are classes and seminars on all of the above all the time, so that if you wanted to study here and absorb Mexico, this would be a fine place to do it.

There is quite a variety of live theater here, including some plays in English. The National Museum of Anthropology is one of the great museums of the world. The Metro (subway) system is top-notch. Public transportation varies from excellent to adequate. Taxis are cheap. Wives of foreign businessmen have associations and support groups that aren't found in many other locations. Medical facilities are first-rate. There is a jai-alai fronton.

Mexico City is a happening place and things get done here, so that it is possible for a businessman to actually fly in and get some work done and fly out the same day. As the center of government and financial power for the country, it is the place to conduct business. There are several golf courses and country clubs.

There are several English-speaking 12 Step groups, including **AA**, **Alanon** and **NA**. There are also meditation groups, self-help groups and groups for a variety of people with special interests. The Newcomers Club and the American Society of Mexico will help new arrivals feel at home. They can be of particular help to the wives of executives transferred here. The **ABC (American British) Hospital is top-notch.**

The American Embassy is located at Paseo de la Reforma 305, Col. Cuauhtémoc, 06500 Mexico, D.F., phone: 211-0042. In these days of terrorism, getting into the embassy is not as easy as it used to be and you will be asked for a passport. If you are going there because you lost yours, you will still be able to get in. The guards speak English.

The Canadian Chancery is at Schiller 529, Col. Polanco, 11580 Mexico, D.F., phone: 724-7900 (mailing address: APDO Postal #105-05, 11580 Mexico, D.F.). Free call from anywhere in Mexico: 91-800-706-29. MITNET: 379-3000. Fax: (Administration) 724-7980, (Public affairs) 724-7981, (Trade) 724-7982, 724-7984, (Immigration) 724-7983, (HOM/Political) 724-7985. MITNET Fax: (Administration) 379-3900, (Public affairs) 379-3904, (Trade) 379-3902, (Immigration) 379-3901, (HOM/Political) 379-3914.

The best source for information about the city and the country is the slick book *Travellers Guide to Mexico,* published in Mexico. You will find it in all the best hotels and at bookstores. Buy a copy if you want to know more about the culture or about doing business in Mexico, or if you intend to do any upscale traveling to the main tourist spots.

The Mexico bureaus of the Associated Press and the *Los Angeles Times* are in the same neighborhood, 295 Reforma. *New Orleans Times-Picayune, The Dallas Morning News, San Antonio Express-News, San Jose (CA) Mercury News, The New York Times* and many more have bureaus in the city.

For the Businessman

U.S. Export Development Office/U.S. Trade Center, 31 Liverpool, 06600 Mexico, D.F., phone: (5) 591-0155.

Mexico City Chamber of Commerce, 42 Reforma, 3rd Floor, 06048 Mexico, D.F., phone: 705-0424.

American Chamber of Commerce of Mexico, 78 Lucerma, Col. Juarez, 06000 Mexico, D.F., phone: 724-3800.

Canadian Chamber of Commerce, Paseo de la Reforma 369, Mezzanine, Col. Cuauhtémoc, 06920 Mexico, D.F., phone: 525-0741.

Additionally, several states have a Chamber of Commerce office or a trade mission:

Arizona—Torre Caballito, 10 Reforma, 7th Floor, Col. Guerrero, 06030 Mexico, D.F., phone: 566-9850, fax: 566-9642.

California—450 Reforma, 4th Floor, Col. Juarez, 06600 Mexico, D.F., phone: 208-5161, fax: 208-5761.

Florida—19 Rio Marne, #203, Col. Cuauhtémoc, 06500 Mexico, D.F., phone: 535-2475, fax: 535-2475.

Illinois—450 Reforma, 4th Floor, Col. Juarez, 06600 Mexico, D.F., phone: 208-4450, fax: 511-2084.

Louisiana—107 Reforma, 12th Floor, Col. Revolución, 06030 Mexico, D.F., phone: 703-3595, fax: 703-2838.

Michigan—Recreo 109, Col. Del Valle, 03100 Mexico, D.F., phone: 524-8650, fax: 524-9676.

New Mexico—57 Florencia, 3rd Floor, Col. Juarez, 06600 Mexico, D.F., phone: 207-7512, fax: 208-5311.

Oregon—Jose María Velasco 67, Col. San Jose Insurgentes, 03900 Mexico, D.F., phone: 660-1104, fax: 593-5982.

Texas—76 Reforma, 15th Floor, Col. Juarez, 06600 Mexico, D.F., phone: 546-8173, fax: 546-4830.

Utah—33 Amberes, Ste. 904, Col. Juarez, 06600 Mexico, D.F., phone: 514-7755, fax: 514-7755.

Wisconsin—Rio Nilo 90, Ste. 604, Col. Cuauhtémoc, 06500 Mexico, D.F., phone: 533-6217, fax: 207-6879.

Jewish Resources

There is a Beth (Ashkenazi, Conservative) Israel Community Center and Synagogue, Blvd. Virreyes 1140, Lomas de Virreyes, phone: 540-2642,

There is a strong Jewish community in Mexico City.

services Fri. 8 P.M. There are also other synagogues and Jewish organizations. Among them are:

Comité Central Israelita de Mexico, Cofre de Perote 115, Lerma, 11000 Mexico, D.F., phone: 540-3273, 540-7376, 520-9393.

Maugen David (Aleppo-Sephardi, Orthodox), Bernard Shaw 10, Polanco, 11570 Mexico, D.F., phone: 280-4727, 280-7456.

Bet Moshe (Shami-Sephardi, Orthodox), Tennyson 134, Polanco, 11560 Mexico, D.F., phone: 280-9956, 281-3969.

There are also kosher restaurants and butchers. You will be able to meet people from all over the world here. Meeting them is not as difficult as it would be in a large U.S. city, though this is not so true for those who are living here. As a tourist, you will meet traveling companions at your hotels, museums, etc. As a resident, you will probably ally yourself with some of the English-language expatriate organizations. There are cultural events and trendy restaurants.

There is just such energy here that you can get sucked into it. I find myself more creative when I'm here, but after a while the adrenaline and energy of twenty-one million souls begins to wear thin.

CONS

Before the devaluation (and probably sometime in the future), Mexico City can be one of the most expensive places in the world in terms of real estate. Rent is comparable to New York, and the quality of what you get will be less.

Buying a place here should only be done if you are absolutely sure that this is where you want to be. It is expensive. For short stays of a few weeks or months, check out the fine "suites hotels" that have living rooms and kitchen facilities. The traffic can be horrible. **Because of the intense traffic, allow an extra hour to get to important business meetings.**

The pollution is indeed as terrible as you have heard. Pollution is still the number one complaint by visitors and residents. It is worst from December to April, when the thermal inversions can trap the pollution in the valley. Places like Bosques do not feel the impact as much as downtown, but it is still there. **Contact lens wearers** will find it uncomfortable after the second day. Bring a spare set of glasses. The traffic police, although they have improved in the past few years, have been backsliding lately. This means that they are still looking for *mordida* (a little bite), or bribe. Unless you absolutely have to, don't rent a car here.

Another new wrinkle is that **car theft** has skyrocketed since the peso devaluation. Just like in the United States, there are people who will point guns at you and take your vehicle. Let them have it. Car theft is a legitimate problem. If you do plan to have your own vehicle here, invest in a Club™ and an alarm system before you go. Park only in a guarded parking lot. Do not leave your purse or other valuables in plain sight in your car while driving.

One scam is that one of the boys who tries to wash your window or sell you something at a traffic light will put a piece of chewing gum or other mark on your car if he sees you have something to steal. His *compadre* at the next light will look for the mark and break a window and grab and run. Daylight assaults are rare, but try not to look too much like a tourist and keep an eye on your surroundings. Pickpockets abound, especially in crowds—which is just about everywhere. The pace and the noise and the people will eventually get to you. That is why so many *Chilangos* (local slang for people who live in Mexico City) escape to Cuernavaca for the weekend. *Chilango* was originally a derogatory term, but many of them use it now, so I don't think it still carries the sting it used to. Still, I wouldn't call someone that to his face unless he had already used the word in conversation.

Until recently, crime in D.F. (as many locals call it, **pronounced "day ef fay"**) was not as bad as in major U.S. cities. Right now, **crime is out of control.** Be very careful. Take only official taxis from taxi stands, or have your hotel concierge call one for you. **Don't be afraid to go there, just don't be stupid** and flash a lot of cash. As far as walking the streets and looking at a map, I have had so many *Chilangos* help me and warn me to be careful, that I am not really afraid to do it. I figure that a crook is going to realize you are a tourist anyway, so why be both paranoid and lost?

Now, a word of **warning for those who like to party late and/or visit ladies of the evening.** You are perfectly safe in the Zona Rosa until midnight or so. After that, there are *Guys, read this!* crooks who prey on staggering drunks of all nationalities. At some clubs it is not unheard of for a hooker or bartender to slip you a Mickey (as opposed to a Mikey, who is never slipped to anyone).

Even if you take a hooker to your room, she could slip you one before she slips out of her slip. **Be wary of any drink (including mineral water) that you do not uncap yourself.** If you are going to stay out late and stumble home, try to do so with a buddy. Just like anywhere else, use your head.

Take a cab from a cab stand, even if you only have a few blocks to go. If you visit the houses of ill repute, find out from a local which ones have a good reputation. You used to be safe in all of them, but not anymore. The good ones do not want trouble and try to keep their employees in line. You may be at risk, however, when you leave, so again, try to go with a buddy.

I have known people who have spent a lot of time in places like this and have never had any problems, but I think they are just lucky. Sometimes the areas of town are not the greatest, and no matter how well policed the bordello is, their wall of safety ends at their property line.

If you are gay, you will have plenty of company here. Please read the above paragraphs. Like in other parts of the world, gays are considered fair game and there are hate crimes. Chance encounters in gay bars carry a little bit more risk than they do at home, because there are some boys who lure infatuated gringos away from the bar and have a *compadre* roll them. Forget about reporting it to the police, and consider yourself lucky if that is all that happens to you.

Special Note for Executives

You should read *Mexico Business* magazine, available at newsstands or by subscription from 3033 Chimney Rock, Ste. 300, Houston, TX 77056; 713-266-0861, fax: 713-266-0980; e-mail: mailbox@MexicoBusiness.com; www.MexicoBusiness.com. This is the most accurate source of what's happening in the business world throughout Mexico.

If you are a businessman, you will have to spend some time here sooner or later. Try to pace yourself. The altitude is high and the air is difficult to breathe. Take dark suits and leave your white shirts at home. Not only will you blend in better, but a white shirt will be gray by the end of the day. Winters are downright chilly. Bring a sweater or wool suit. Topcoats are probably gilding the lily, but if you are cold-natured, you could sometimes need one. Summers are hot. Short sleeves are gaining acceptance, but for first meetings you should still wear long sleeves underneath your suit. If you are going to be here a week or so, consider one of the suites hotels instead of a regular hotel. The regular hotels are as expensive as sin. If you are a visible corporate executive, the possibility of kidnapping exists. This is only true for very high-level persons and should not be a worry for mid-level business travelers. I mention this partly to reassure some who may be afraid to travel here and to be honest about a problem that could affect a small number of foreigners.

Some very rich Mexicans and foreigners have been the targets of kidnappers (like in other places in the world, including the United States). They have taken precautions like hiring personal security personnel. If you have this high a visibility, your company has probably already given you a seminar by one of these companies. You should follow their advice. They may be a little paranoid, but that is their business. Your personnel office should be able to direct you to reputable companies. If they are unaware of any, have them contact their counterparts in Mexico City and/or the U.S. Embassy or the Canadian Chancery in Mexico City. The rest of us are not worth the effort and have as much to worry about from international terrorists in Mexico as we do in Des Moines.

IN-BETWEENS

If you are a journalist in Mexico, Mexico City is the place to be. By the same token, if you are a freelancer, you will find living here a mixed bag. Don't move here without having a good number of contacts before you leave. Developing contacts with U.S. or Canadian editors, art directors, etc., is difficult at best and expensive as all get out. Learn to depend on your fax machine and send messages at night. **Get on the Net.** Learn to judge how urgent it is to talk to them. Shorts can be worn by both men and women, but most Mexicans wear slacks or jeans. Artistic types will find a lot to do here. This is the art capital of Mexico.

Housing

There is no getting around it—this is an expensive town. If you are on an expense account, make sure your accountant isn't living in the dark ages (ten years ago) when living here was reasonable. An executive-style apartment is going to cost a bare minimum of $1,200 a month. You can easily spend a lot more if you want things like security, a quiet neighborhood and good air. If you are only going to be here a few months, consider one of the "suites hotels." They offer kitchen facilities and a living room.

It may take you a few months to find a place anyway. A journalist friend of mine spent two months finding a place she could afford (she worked on the *News*—not noted for its high pay). She had to commute an hour to work and take a cab at night. If you are looking for an apartment and speak a little Spanish, get a publication called *Segundomano* (Secondhand). It comes out on Tuesdays and Fridays and is full of classifieds (that's all it has) and is the number one way to find an apartment in Mexico City. If you are looking for a dog, cat, pen pal or other things, they are in there too. You may find your place in the English-language papers, but many of the choice places do not advertise in any paper, English or Spanish. Another alternative is to put an ad in both English and Spanish newspapers.

The Polanco section, or Lomas, are considered the ideal choices, if you can afford them. Other sections are Anzures, Coyoacan and San Angel. Many of the other colonies are perfectly acceptable and less expensive, so check around.

✪ *Cuernavaca, Morelos*

Altitude:	5,058 ft.
Population:	More than 1,000,000
Climate:	Perfect all year.
Housing:	All price ranges.
Ambiente:	Cultured. A good mix of Mexicans and foreigners.
Medical care:	Excellent.
Area code:	73

PROS

God must have been trying to make the perfect climate when He created Cuernavaca. It never gets too hot or too cold. The rains in the rainy season fall mainly at night. This nurtures some of the most beautiful gardens and golf courses in the world. Indeed, Cuernavaca is famous for its gardens, in particular the Borda Gardens. For those who need a moist climate in order to breathe, such as someone who has had an operation on his larynx, this is the ideal location. Although it is a city of more than a million people, there is a peace and tranquillity here that makes you forget that. This city is **cosmopolitan** enough to satisfy any taste. There are restaurants of almost all nationalities here. The *zócalo,* or main square, is alive day and night with activity. In the evenings, there are often free band concerts. The sidewalk cafes are great places to sit and watch the world go by, or to meet new and old acquaintances. There are seven golf courses in the neighborhood.

There is plenty of housing, ranging from condos, to exclusive communities, to new developments specifically built for foreigners, to rentals in all price ranges, to simple dwellings. There is an RV park south of town. There is **English AA.** There are hot springs nearby and two spas in town. There is an archeological site in the city, Pirámide de Teopanzolco. Medical care is very good, with hospitals and doctors aplenty, many of whom speak English.

There are two **spas** in the city, Hosteria las Quintas (which is my favorite in Mexico) and the Misión del Sol, which has a New Age, **spiritual ambiance** including a **Zen** meditation center. Speaking of spirituality, there must be a lot of it in the neighborhood. The old Barbara Hutton estate (now the Camino Real Sumiya) has a Zen meditation garden and a prayer temple. Misión del Sol spa and resort qualifies as a spiritual retreat. (See my book *Spas & Hot Springs of Mexico* for more details or call 1-800-321-4622 to get a brochure.)

Many artists and writers have found the intellectual climate here to be stimulating. The foreign population doesn't overwhelm the city. You really feel like you are in old colonial Mexico here. The art and architecture here give you an appreciation for the history of the country.

The Museo de Cuauhnahuac, in the Cortés Palace, has a Diego Rivera mural and a comprehensive history of Mexico through the colonial period. The Museo Casa Robert Brady exhibits over 1,200 works of art from pre-Hispanic to colonial to modern. Works of Rufino Tamayo and Frida Kahlo are on display. Handicrafts from all over the world are also exhibited. A unique museum for those who are interested in herbs is the Museo de la Herbolaría, which was established to preserve and promote traditional folk medicine. Communications are excellent and Internet access is available.

There is a local foreign resident library, the Guild House, at Tuxtla Gutierrez #111. They also have activities for foreigners and information about other foreign societies like the Center for Creative Arts, the American Legion, the Navy League and the American Benevolent Society.

Language Schools

There are several language schools here and they are very good. In my opinion, they are better than those in San Miguel de Allende, perhaps because the atmosphere here is different and you are forced to use your fledgling language skills. Two are: The Center for Bilingual Multicultural Studies, San Jeronimo #304 (mailing address: APDO Postal #1520, 62000 Cuernavaca, Mor.), phone: (73) 17-1087; and there is the Universal Centro de Lengua y Comunicacion Social, H. Preciado #332 (mailing address: APDO Postal #1-1826, 62000 Cuernavaca, Mor.), phone: (73) 18-2904, 12-4902.

CONS

There aren't many. Some may find this too big a city for them. Others may consider the weekend intrusion of thousands of people from Mexico City a nuisance. If you are looking for a place to get away from it all, this isn't it. It is not for those truly on a strict budget, though lower-cost housing is available, as in any city, but you will have to look hard for it.

IN-BETWEENS

This has been a popular retirement community for decades. It is also popular with U.S. students who have exchange classes with the university here.

◎ *Morelia, Michoacán*

Altitude:	6,400 ft.
Population:	450,000
Climate:	Cool summers, moderate winters.
Housing:	Adequate in all price ranges.
Ambiente:	Cultured, old colonial charm for a big city.
Medical care:	Good.
Area code:	43

PROS

It will cost **less to live here** than many other places. The weather is very nice and pretty constant all year, though it can get a little chilly (jacket weather) during the winter. It never gets too hot. It is a very cultured, conservative city, and there are plays, concerts and various activities at the university. You could attend the university to take language courses. Hint—if you sign up in town, the course will cost about $50. If you sign up through a U.S. university, you will pay several hundred dollars. I met a middle-aged guy here who was living on $150 a month, renting a room in a house and going to school.

The zoo, modeled after the San Diego Zoo, is excellent. Nearby are some very interesting towns (Pátzcuaro, Villa Escalante, Santa Clara del Cobre and more) noted for crafts and natural beauty. You will not be overwhelmed by other gringos living here. There are a lot of cultural activities here, including plays and concerts and other highbrow events. The atmosphere is very Spanish and you truly get the feeling of living in colonial Mexico. There is an RV park and there are plenty more in nearby Pátzcuaro. In fact, that might be a better choice. There is a golf course.

CONS

The conservative atmosphere will not appeal to everyone. If your lifestyle is at all nonconservative, then you had best skip this city. There is a strong social society here. Although you will be able to make friends here as well as in any conservative town, you will have a long way to go to be part of the social scene that makes the newspapers, if that is important to you. There is no English-language AA, but many Mexican groups.

IN-BETWEENS

Because Morelia is halfway between Mexico City and Guadalajara, both by the toll road and the old road, getting here is easy by car. There are no direct flights from the United States, but many from Mexico City. If you simply want a place to be and observe as a third party, rather than be assimilated into either a Mexican or expatriate community, this could be your place.

◉ *Pátzcuaro, Michoacán*

Altitude:	6,977 ft.
Population:	55,000
Climate:	Cool summers, moderate winters.
Housing:	Adequate in all price ranges.
Ambiente:	Very conservative, small-town mentality. Few gringos in residence.
Medical care:	Good.
Area code:	43

PROS

Quiet, situated on a placid lake just about sums it up. Prices are **inexpensive**. There are several RV parks to choose from, one of which is right on the lake. The weather in the summer is very nice, and in the winter it is only mildly chilly. There is good trout fishing all around. There are a few "in" places where you can hear traditional music. The food is decent, especially the local delicacy: whitefish from the lake.

If you are interested in crafts, you could learn a lot from the Indians, who are famous for their wood carving and their lacquerware. The masks from here are superb. There is a real atmosphere of old, backwater Mexico here. If you want to get away from it all, you can do it here.

CONS

See the last sentence of the above paragraph. There are very few foreigners here, though there are quite a few tourists. The small-town atmosphere can get to you after a while. Some say the lake is contaminated, so I wouldn't eat too many of the whitefish.

IN-BETWEENS

There aren't any. You either love the place or hate it.

The South

Oaxaca, Oaxaca

Altitude:	5,069 ft.
Population:	210,000
Climate:	Mild all year; take a jacket for evenings.
Housing:	Less expensive than most, a little scarce.
Ambiente:	Conservative, old-world, international, Indian, cultured.
Medical care:	Adequate.
Area code:	952

PROS

If you want to **get away from it all,** this is almost as far away as you can get (San Cristobal, Chiapas, is farther). If you are interested in weaving, pottery, archeology, Indian culture, traditional Mexico as it was a century ago, Oaxaca is for you. It has been called the craft capital of Mexico.

Oaxaca is one of Mexico's colonial cities and has one of the largest Saturday markets in the country. The sidewalk cafes give the city a European charm and the locals are quite friendly. A real treat is visiting the nearby villages. Each has its own craft specialty: rugs, pottery, linens, hand-carved wooden animals and more.

The weather is essentially **springlike** all year (some say perfect), though a sweater or light jacket will come in handy. You can hang around the *zócalo* and watch people from all over the world walk by. You can also see various political demonstrations, as this has been a hotbed of political thought since before the Revolution. Don't take this the wrong way—it is more like Berkeley, California, or Austin, Texas, than a more conservative city, that's all.

Housing costs (separate from schools) are less than most other places in this book. You can rent a luxury home for about $1,000 and simple digs for about $250.

There are cultural activities ranging from piano recitals to plays to folk dances. There are more European and Asian tourists than Americans. There is a good English-language library, the Biblioteca Circulante, Alcala 305. If you stay here, you should donate your time and/or your money to them. There is little in the way of organized English-speaking AA, though there are some English-speaking loners. Check at the lending library for meetings. Many artists have settled here. There is a U.S. consular agent: Mark Arnold Leyes, Alcala #201 Desp. 206, 68000 Oaxaca, Oax., phone/fax: (951) 4-3054. The Canadian consul is at: 119 Dr. Liceaga #8, 68000 Oaxaca, Oax. (mailing address: The Consulate of Canada, APDO Postal #29A Sucursal C, Col. Reforma, 68050 Oaxaca, Oax.), phone: (011-52-322) 33-777, fax: (011-52-322) 52-147. Honorary Consul: Ms. F. May. Territory includes the states of Oaxaca and Chiapas.

Language Schools

There are some Spanish-language schools here that are quite good: Instituto Cultural Oaxaca, 900 Av. Juarez, phone: (951) 5-3404, fax: (951) 6-1382; and the Universidad Autónoma Benito Juarez, 127 Angeles Clemente Circuito Norte, Fracc. La Cascada, CP 68040, phone: (952) 6-5922. The man who ran the former died several years ago and I have heard his wife is trying to keep it going. It is famous for a course in Oaxacan cooking. The latter also offers courses for college credits as well as individual classes for those who just want to learn.

CONS

The very **isolation** that makes Oaxaca so different may be a minus in the eyes of many peoples. It is a good three or four days' drive from the Texas border. There are a few flights from Mexico City. The town is very conservative. You should watch your wallet or purse in the markets.

IN-BETWEENS

There has always been an expatriate community of **individualists** and artists in this city. Their numbers have never been great, perhaps 100. There are only about 300 foreigners in the entire state. If you are into Indian arts and crafts, though, you couldn't find a better place to learn about them. The archeology sites in the area are excellent.

❂ *Pto. Escondido, Oaxaca*

Altitude:	Not much.
Population:	5,000
Climate:	Absolutely perfect, except May–Sept., when it rains a lot and is fairly hotter than normal (but cooler than most of the United States). Deliciously pleasant spring, fall and winter.
Housing:	Plenty of low-cost places, some middle-class houses.
Ambiente:	Bohemian to escapee chic. Lots of gringos in winter. Laid-back, tropical.
Medical care:	Barely adequate.
Area code:	956

PROS

I used to live here and if I ever "retire" again, I would certainly consider it. The beach is absolutely gorgeous, with a medium-grain golden sand (smoother than Acapulco) and the **biggest waves in Mexico.** It is the site of the national surf competition and there are surfers from around the world who make a pilgrimage here to the "Mexican Pipeline." You can swim any time of the year.

There are a variety of tourists, from the chic who have "discovered" the place to the hippie backpackers who soon leave because it is "too touristy." They head on down to Pto. Angel. The sizable Italian community gives the place an international flair and a good choice in restaurants.

The **fishing** is excellent—tuna, snapper, billfish. You can buy fresh fish from the fishermen on the beach. There is a contingent of Americans and Canadians who regularly spend their winters here, so there is some continuity of society. They are generally in their thirties to fifties. If you are a **bohemian,** you will find a wide variety of places to live, from rooms atop restaurants to *cabañas* on the beach. Your neighbors will likely be surfers or other bohemians. A musician friend of mine, Joe "King" Carrasco, spent some very creative months here. There is a **topless beach.**

CONS

There is no real "community." If you desire the company of other foreigners year-round, it will be hard. In the winter that will be no problem, but during the rest of the year you will be alone. There is a transient, beach-town atmosphere about the place. There are **no medical facilities** to speak of, although there are enough doctors and dentists for routine care. Be careful about choosing your habitat—make sure you are downwind from the discos. **Summer is hot as the devil—and then it rains and rains and rains.** Like any beach town, it tolerates a certain amount of promiscuity and gays, but only barely. The people who run the town are basically conservative. Communications are not always dependable. There is no English AA, but there is a Spanish-speaking group that is very friendly.

The scuba diving is okay, but nothing to write home about. The snorkeling is just as good. The biggest thing to do in the early evening is to watch the sunset, either from the outside restaurant of the Santa Fe, the classiest hotel in town, or from the rocks out beyond the airport. There was a young couple who had (or maybe still have) an Indian sweat lodge and **spiritual center** with massage, Patricia Heuze and Alejandro Villanueva, Av. Infraganti #28, Col. Lázaro Cárdenas, phone: 2-0908. Things like this come and go, so I can't say for sure they will still be there when you arrive. I hope so. I wrote my first unpublished novel here, so the atmosphere is conducive to writing—if you can avoid the all-night partying that is pervasive.

✪ *Pto. Angel, Oaxaca*

Altitude:	Yes, if you climb a hill.
Population:	1,000
Climate:	Hot as hell and rainy in the summer. Perfect in the winter.
Housing:	Scarce, except for bohemian digs. Cheap.
Ambiente:	*Really* laid-back. Bohemian. It's a fishing village.
Medical care:	Substandard.
Area code:	956

PROS

Bohemians love this place. It is so far off the beaten track that you will think you have gone back in time to the sixties. This may fade after a time, but who knows? You can rent a thatched-roof *cabaña* on the beach or just a place to hang your hammock right by the ocean for a few dollars a day. There is a totally nude beach, frequented by Europeans. **Living here is cheap.**

If you are into roughing it and getting away from it all, this is the place for you. There are some regular houses to rent if you really look, and there is always the possibility of renting a cabin long-term at the Posada Cañon Devata, the most interesting place in town. There is no English AA, but there is a Spanish group. The beaches are stupendous and the town is hillier than Pto. Escondido.

CONS

This is not the place for the average "retiree." There are no medical facilities, though there is a doctor or two. As with any small Mexican seaside town, if you have a serious emergency, your best option for medical care is at the naval base. The bohemians can get on one's nerves. Communications are spotty. The pigs in the street, which are quaint at first, can become a real turnoff after a while. If you are not into roughing it, this is a place you should avoid.

IN-BETWEENS

If you are just looking for a place to hang out for a while, this could be okay. A long-term stay would be attractive only to a very special type of person.

The Yucatán

Cancún, Quintana Roo

Altitude:	None.
Population:	400,000
Climate:	Absolutely perfect, except May—Sept., when it rains and rains, and hurricanes may blow you away. While it is warmer than normal at this time, it is still cooler than most of the United States.
Housing:	Prices have dropped in recent years so that, if you stay away from the tourist zone, you can live decently here for less than in San Miguel or Chapala—or even Playa del Carmen.
Ambiente:	Hedonistic. Party-till-you-drop mentality. Rather like Miami Beach.
Medical care:	Very good.
Area code:	98

PROS

Cancún was created from a computer model by the Mexican government. They inputted what American tourists wanted from a vacation, and the location, with its white sand, tropical atmosphere and accessibility (if they built an airport), came up. While there were a few resident fishermen living in the area, the town was built from scratch. Consequently, it was built with a purified water system and brand-new pipes. They did this rather than modernize existing villages because they wanted to create a sterile environment to attract the tourists who did not appreciate Mexico. Of course, the fact that some prominent politicians could buy up the land before the development began might have had something to do with it too.

The beaches are beautiful, with powder-white sand surrounded by crystal-clear turquoise water. The discos are full of beautiful people. English is spoken almost everywhere. You can get *The New York Times, Miami Herald* and *USA Today* daily. There are brokerage houses. Communications are excellent. There are two 18-hole golf courses. There are American-style condos.

Cancún is a tourist's paradise with sprawling white-sand beaches, crystal-clear water, a modernized plumbing system and English spoken everywhere.

There is plenty of American-style food from familiar chains. There are direct flights to the United States, Canada and Europe. The weather is perfect. There is a good-sized regular **AA and Alanon** community with daily meetings. There is an RV park out of town. The American consular agent is at: Lorraine H. Lara, Av. Nadar 40-super Manzana 2A Edificio Marruecos, 3rd floor #31, 77500 Cancún, Q.R., phone: (98) 84-2411, 84-6399, fax: (98) 84-8222. The Canadian consul is at: The Consulate of Canada, Centro Comercial Plaza Mexico, Local 312, Av. Tulum, 200 Esq. Agua, 77500 Cancún, Q.R., phone: (011-52-98) 84-3716, fax: (011-52-98) 62420. Honorary Consul: Mr. O. Lavole. Territory includes the states of Campeche Yucatán and Quintana Roo.

The scuba is great. The snorkeling is great. The fishing is great. Medical care is very good. There are hospitals. The water is purified out of the tap.

CONS

It is as **expensive** as the dickens. The economy is based on the dollar, so you do not get to take advantage of any fluctuations. The place has no real soul. You will soon wonder if you are even in Mexico, until you try to do business. There are so many Ugly Americans that you will be ashamed to be from the same country.

IN-BETWEENS

It is a great town for **business,** a real Babbittville. There are some very pretty areas nearby to escape to. My favorite is Isla Mujeres. There is a bullring. The town is gay-friendly.

❂ *Playa del Carmen, Quintana Roo*

Altitude:	None.
Population:	60,000; 500–600 foreign residents, many Italians
Climate:	Absolutely perfect, except May–Sept., when it rains and rains, and hurricanes may blow you away. While it is warmer than normal at this time, it is still cooler than most of the United States.
Housing:	Remarkably expensive. More expensive than Cancún because of the lack of availability. The Playacar section has lots of modern condos.
Ambiente:	No longer a hippie haven, it is rather upscale. Still hedonistic. Lots of party animals hang out (and get hung over) here.
Medical care:	Barely adequate, but Cancún is nearby for emergencies.
Area code:	98

PROS

The beaches are lovely. The atmosphere is **laid-back.** There is enough development so that you won't feel like you are on a primitive isle, but at the same time, you won't feel overwhelmed like you were in Cancún. The atmosphere is funky, with room for every lifestyle, from the hippie hanging out to the rich retiree who spends all his time making more money. The snorkeling and scuba are excellent. There is such a variety of tourists, including many Europeans, that you will always have someone to talk to. If you are a bohemian, you will fit in. If you are single, you won't have to stay that way for long. Costs are less than Cancún. There is a **topless beach.**

CONS

The **transient** nature of the place will get to you after a while. There is a small community of expatriates and you will soon make their acquaintance. The fall storms can be a really unpleasant experience. There is now regular **English AA** at the Playacar School, Ave. 10, just down from the Continental Plaza Hotel. Tell the gate guard you are going to *doub lay ah* (AA). Finding digs will take some digging. Because it is a small town and there are a lot of foreigners, there is not much supply. What is available tends to be expensive. You can, however, find real budget places. There is not an RV park to speak of, although there is a very small one near the beach.

IN-BETWEENS

It's laid-back, no doubt about it. You could probably write a great novel here. I know I could. It is close enough to Cancún to enable you to have everything you need and far enough away to have a different flavor. It's not for everyone, but it is great for those who like it.

✪ Xcalac, Quintana Roo

Altitude:	None.
Population:	600
Climate:	Absolutely perfect, except May–Sept., when it rains and rains, and hurricanes may blow you away. While it is warmer than normal at this time, it is still cooler than most of the United States.
Housing:	Scarce and primitive. Wind generators supply most of the power.
Ambiente:	Hedonistic. Party-till-you-drop mentality. Rather like Miami Beach.
Medical care:	Very good.
Area code:	98

PROS

You can **really get away from it all** here—for now. This little fishing village, stuck like an afterthought onto the peninsula that juts down toward Belize at the tip of Mexico, is gorgeous. The beaches are not quite as nice as Cancún, but the coral reefs are magnificent. The **scuba** is world-class here, some say better than Cozumel. It is here that I learned to dive.

The **Chinchorro Banks** are just offshore and they are teeming with fish. The **fishing** is also magnificent here, for tarpon, permit and many more game fish, both in the bays and out in the blue water. You can really enjoy the nature and quiet at night.

There's not a lot to the town, and there are (presently) only a few small hotels and condominiums that do not detract from the natural beauty. The foreign community has not overwhelmed the native community and they coexist in harmony. If I were to retire, this would be one of my first picks. You could write or paint great things here.

CONS

This place is really isolated. **Medical care is inadequate.** If you get really sick, you will have to go to Chetumal or Cancún for treatment. Communications are spotty. The very isolation that attracted you may wear thin after a while. There is no English AA.

IN-BETWEENS

All of the above will change. Only by the grace of God will this unspoiled paradise retain its character. This outpost of serenity will not last and it is not my fault for including it in this book. Progress is inevitable and no place in a perfect setting can remain isolated forever. The international interests and Cancún businessmen have already bought large tracts of land for developments that will irrevocably change the atmosphere of the area.

There is a land boom going on, similar to the one in Pto. Escondido in the eighties when I lived there. The airport has grown a terminal, perhaps presaging a case of terminal development. There is a new highway going in that will bypass the sand road that bumps and grinds its way to the village after you turn off the main road that leads from the highway. The five-hour drive from Cancún will be shortened to four hours.

I don't mean to be a Gloomy Gus. **These changes will make life better for those who actually live here and will enable more people like you and me to appreciate the area.** It will not become "another Cancún," but it will become something that it isn't today. There are people who moan about several other places in this book that have been "ruined" by development. I am not so arrogant that I want a beautiful area all to myself. I can only pray that the developers pursue their goal with consideration. There will always be unspoiled places—they will just be harder to get to.

If you want to invest in the area, I can think of no one better to suggest than my friend Andy (Scuba Daddy) Sanders, phone: 011-52-983-80404. He has his finger on the pulse of the area and can tell you what is a good deal and what to avoid. I trust him.

The Pacific Coast

❁ Acapulco, Guerrero

Altitude:	In the hills.
Population:	800,000
Climate:	Winters are divine. Summers are devilish, with rain and heat. It rains in Sept. or throughout hurricane season.
Housing:	A wide choice from super-luxury to super-simple.
Ambiente:	Big-city glitz, discos, beaches. Sensual, tropical.
Medical care:	Very good.
Area code:	74

PROS

Ah, Acapulco! The very name conjures up images of **steamy sensuality,** beautiful people and beautiful beaches. All of these are realities. The place is a veritable cornucopia of pleasures of the senses. The **beaches,** some long and sweeping, some tiny and private, have lured tourists from all over the world for many years.

Acapulco is truly tropical, with palm trees, coconut groves, mangos and flowers of every imaginable color screaming for your attention. The **winter weather is heavenly.** It is very **cosmopolitan,** with world-class shopping and Wal-Marts and the occasional *tienda* sandwiched in between.

The yacht crowd likes it, the rich and famous like it, the Duke liked it and Arnold the Incredible likes it. Many movies have been shot here and more will be. It has the only jai-alai fronton on the mainland, besides Mexico City.

The city is large enough that it offers an incredible **diversity of housing,** ranging from the very, very rich suburbs to downright hovels that would be cheap enough for anyone's budget. There is **English AA, and Alanon** too. U.S. newspapers are readily available. Communications are basically good, except when it rains they become sporadic. There are RV parks, from one across from the beach on the busy *Costera* (main drag) to inexpensive ones way out in the country to one right on the beach in quiet Pie de la Cuesta, an hour away. The nightlife is superb, if modern music à la disco is your bag. The annual music festival attracts musicians from around the world.

There is an American consular agent at the Hotel Club del Sol, Costera Miguel Aleman Esq. Reyes Católicos, 19300 Acapulco, Gro., phone: (74) 85-7207, 85-6600, fax: (74) 85-7207. There is also a small English-language newspaper. There is an American Legion Post.

There is a Canadian consulate: The Consulate of Canada, Hotel Club del Sol, Costera Miguel Aleman Esq. Reyes Católicos, Acapulco, Gro. Mailing address: The Consulate of Canada, APDO Postal #94-C, 39300 Acapulco, Gro., phone: (011-52-74) 85-6621, fax: (011-52-74) 86-7417. Honorary Consul: Mrs. D. McLean. Territory includes the states of Guerrero and Michoacán.

You can **choose your lifestyle** here, from the Gold Zone, where most of the high-rise hotels are, to the old section around the *zócalo,* which is seedy and has a real flavor of seaport Mexico, to the exclusive subdivisions out by Las Brisas or the Princess Marquesa with its world-class golf course.

There's an international airport with flights from around the world. There are enough French and German tourists that you could hang out with a European crowd if you wanted. There are Internet connections. The food is outstanding. The variety of restaurants is overwhelming—from five-star gourmet palaces to funky palapas serving inexpensive seafood. There is scuba diving, though the Pacific cannot compete with the clear waters of the Yucatan. Medical care is adequate and there are hospitals here. Sounds great, huh? Then why don't more foreigners live here?

CONS

The **summer is beastly.** It is hot and humid. It rains every day. The phones go out. Although the city has done an admirable job of cleaning up, it still has a way to go. The traffic is fast and **noisy.** It goes all night. Even in the high-rise Gold Zone hotels, I have a hard time sleeping.

There is a sense of impermanence to this place, due to the transient nature of tourism. Acapulco is a big city. The foreign community is tiny, unless you are rich enough to hang out with the Las Brisas crowd. If you are, you will find plenty of friends. If you are not, you will not. The water is beautiful. However, even though the city has installed a sewage treatment facility, the runoffs from the slums above the city still make some parts of the beaches questionable. The **English AA** is small except during the winter.

IN-BETWEENS

You can speak **English or Spanish or French** here and someone will always understand you. You can **party all night** if you want. The discos don't really get rocking until after midnight. Then you could lie on the beach and recuperate. You could write a great book here, but the temptations of the flesh would make it hard. You sense that a Graham Greene–like ghost haunts the older section. It is a very **libertine town**. It is quite **gay-friendly**. There are clubs and social organizations for you. Its size makes lots of things available, but getting around is a pain. The smallness of the foreign community could force you to assimilate yourself into the Mexican society.

☼ *Pie de la Cuesta, Guerrero*

Altitude:	Sea level.
Population:	4,000
Climate:	Winters are divine. Summers are devilish, with rain and heat. It rains in Sept. or throughout hurricane season.
Housing:	Primitive, limited.
Ambiente:	Laid-back, funky beach town.
Medical care:	Primitive.
Area code:	74

PROS

Only about an hour away, this small beach and fishing village is almost like **something out of a South Seas novel**. James Michener would approve. It is quiet and serene. You are far removed from the hustle and bustle of Acapulco. Housing should be quite reasonable. There is a first-class RV park and a couple of very nice, inexpensive ones on the beach. The food is great.

CONS

You had better like **isolation**. This is a small village with few full-time foreign residents. The very things that attracted you to this locale wear thin after a while. Medical care is rudimentary. If you get really sick, you will have to go to Acapulco.

I don't want to give the village a bad rap, as so many guidebooks have done, because the ocean is a changeable thing. The beach is stupendous, the sunsets are legendary and the swimming is, *at times,* dangerous. The waves are larger than Acapulco's and the undertow can be fierce. Ask the locals what the situation is like before you jump in. I swam there and enjoyed it, and there are times when I won't put my big toe in the water.

IN-BETWEENS

You could **write a great novel here.** If you are truly independent and **self-sufficient,** you might find it to be a perfect place. Little English is spoken, so you will be forced to learn some Spanish. It's a unique place and not for everyone. There is little, if any, full-time foreign community.

✺ *Manzanillo, Colima*

Altitude:	In the hills.
Population:	80,000
Climate:	Warm winters. Hot, humid summers.
Housing:	From simple apartments to middle-class condos near the beach to gated communities in Nuevo Vallarta.
Ambiente:	Varied—there are artists and writers, retired businesspeople.
Medical care:	Good.
Area code:	322

PROS

Manzanillo has a **very Mexican** *ambiente.* That is probably its draw to those who love it, and there are plenty of foreigners who love it. The city is an important port and has industry enough to keep it from being dependent on the tourist trade to survive. The port, fishing and mining industries are the backbone of the place. **Housing is reasonable** for a beach community and you have a choice of RV parks, condos or houses that range from the luxurious, including gated communities, to the simple.

Although it is good-sized, Manzanillo still feels like a small town. It is close enough to Guadalajara to make a trip there for culture or material acquisition a viable alternative. It is pretty, with nice beaches. The weather is marvelous in winter. The fishing is top-notch, with dorado, marlin, sailfish and more. There are even supposed to be some coral reefs offshore, but I have not seen them. There is a golf course. The seafood is excellent. Communications are excellent. There are adequate medical facilities and a hospital.

CONS

On weekends Manzanillo gets crowded with *Tapatios,* or people from Guadalajara. Someone from New Orleans could live here in summer, but most of us would find it sweltering, just like Vallarta. There is little culture.

IN-BETWEENS

The foreign community is small enough that it doesn't overwhelm the town. Manzanillo maintains a very Mexican flavor and there generally is not a lot of English spoken.

⊙ *Pto. Vallarta, Jalisco*

Altitude:	The nearby Sierra Madres have all you could want.
Population:	260,000
Climate:	Winters—heavenly. Summers—devilish. Humid.
Housing:	Plenty of choices. More expensive than Mazatlán, less than Chapala.
Ambiente:	Sophisticated, charming.
Medical care:	Good.
Area code:	322

PROS

It's hard not to like Vallarta, as the locals call it. This city on the Pacific Ocean was immortalized (or was that immoralized?) by Richard Burton and Elizabeth Taylor when they filmed *Night of the Iguana* there. BI (Before *Iguana*) it was a tucked-away backwater. AI (After *Iguana*) it became a chic place for the Hollywood crowd. It still attracts a chic crowd, though not like it used to. There is a **sizable expat community** here, with a character completely different from Chapala or San Miguel.

The average foreign resident is **younger** than in Chapala. There are more people who simply wanted to live in Mexico and found this to be a perfect place for it. You have your divorcees living on their settlements, youngish couples who have sold businesses in the States, artists and writers who make a living by their wits. There is also a contingent of older retirees who have lived here for many years and wouldn't think of living anywhere else. There are two golf courses.

The temperature is nearly perfect in the winter, though somewhat humid. It can be beastly hot and humid in the summer. There are several cafes that come and go and provide a gathering place for the foreign community while they are around. There are some great chefs here, including John Huston's former chef. John loved the place and there is a statue of him in town. There are art galleries by the score and a very literate crowd, both foreigners and Mexicans. The scenery is majestic, with low mountains covered with dense tropical vegetation meeting the sea (locals call it a jungle, but that is a stretch).

The blue Pacific rolls on endlessly, and if you can afford an ocean-view house or condo, do it. Because the town is built on several hills, you can actually find real houses with good views of the ocean. The cobblestone streets add charm. Housing prices are all over the board. You can spend a fortune on a luxury villa, a fair amount for a condo in town, a small fortune for a house in Nuevo Vallarta with a golf course and gated community or you can rent a place in town inexpensively or pay through the nose for an ocean view. The town is large enough and there is enough choice to make finding some sort of abode relatively easy. The water supply has been officially declared potable by the secretary of health. Many expats still use purified water, because of the old pipes running to their houses. Ask locally.

There is very **strong AA and Alanon** here, with daily meetings. There is plenty of nightlife, from discos to jazz clubs. The town is very **gay-friendly** and there is a sizable gay community.

There are good communications with the outside world. English-language newspapers are available. There is a weekly supplement to the Guadalajara English-language paper, the *Colony Reporter,* and it will keep you up-to-date on the goings-on around Vallarta. Angela Corelis is a reporter for them and she has a most engaging style. You should read the paper, if only for her observations.

Internet connections are available. There are plenty of doctors and a hospital. There is an international airport with direct flights to the United States.

There is a U.S. consular agent here: Jeannette McGill, Parian del Puente (Libertad and Miramar), Local 12-A, 48300 Pto. Vallarta, Jal., phone: (322) 2-0069, fax: (322) 3-0074. Mailing address: APDO Postal #462, Pto. Vallarta, Jal. There is a Canadian consulate: The Consulate of Canada, Calle Hidalgo 226, 160 Zaragoza, Interior 10, Col. Centro, 46300 Pto. Vallarta, Jal., phone: (011-52-322) 253-98, fax: (011-52-322) 235-17. Honorary Consul: Ms. L. Benoit. Territory includes Pto. Vallarta, Jalisco Coast and the states of Colima and Nayarit.

CONS

The beaches near town are not very good for swimming. The beach itself is rocky. The summers are awful. It may not be hell, but the Devil must have a condo there. The cobblestone streets are rough on your car's suspension. There is always the chance of a hurricane or earthquake, though the former is pretty unlikely. Vallarta is usually spared. With earthquakes you never know. There is so much English spoken that it is easy to avoid learning Spanish.

IN-BETWEENS

The foreign community is quite tight-knit. There are plenty of opportunities to get involved in the social scene. There are several worthwhile charity projects where you could donate your time.

❂ Melaque, San Patricio, Bucerias, Rincon de Guayabitos, Jal.

Altitude:	All are at sea level.
Population:	Estimates vary wildly, probably under 2,000 each.
Climate:	Winters—heavenly. Summers—devilish. Humid.
Housing:	Primitive, lots of RV spaces and choices.
Ambiente:	Small seaside fishing villages.
Medical care:	Inadequate, except at naval hospitals for emergencies.
Area code:	322

PROS

I have bundled these beach communities **southeast and northeast of Vallarta** together, because, while they are all different, they are also somewhat similar. You will have to visit each one to determine which *ambiente* appeals to you. They are all **less expensive** than Vallarta to live in, though none of them has the luxury or sophistication of their big sister. They are all somewhat sleepy villages with little in the way of services, but lots in the way of natural beauty.

If you want to **get away from it all,** but not too far away, these towns might be for you. In any of them, you are never too far from a beautiful beach with golden-white sand, palm trees and a riot of tropical vegetation. Housing is reasonable and RV parks are plentiful. Yachtsmen frequently anchor in their harbors and spend some time ashore, so you have an interesting mix of people.

CONS

These are **really small towns.** There is not a large foreign community. There are few activities other than fishing and sunning, so you may get bored. Medical care is minimal. Communications are not always reliable. The summers are beastly.

IN-BETWEENS

If you are an **artist or writer** and want to get away from the madding crowd, these places could be ideal. If you need to socialize with other gringos, you will have enough company during the winter, but otherwise you will be pretty lonely. If you want to learn Spanish, you will have plenty of opportunities to practice, as not much English is spoken.

❂ *San Blas, Nayarit*

Altitude:	Sea level.
Population:	Estimated at 4,000
Climate:	Winters—heavenly. Summers—devilish. Humid.
Housing:	A fair amount at reasonable prices.
Ambiente:	Funky; 1960s hippies still here; lots of backpackers.
Medical care:	Inadequate, except at naval hospitals for emergencies.
Area code:	328

PROS

Thanks, no doubt, to some hyperbolic travel writers, most people have heard of San Blas. There is a small foreign community here, mostly in the winter. It is a **laid-back fishing village.** Housing is cheap. There are RV parks, practically deserted in summer. There is a hot spring nearby. The fishing is good. The seafood is good. Food is cheap. The people who gravitate to this place are cheap. Locals still promenade around the square at night.

With cheap housing, good fishing, great birding and a general carefree way of life, San Blas is one of the most laid back and quiet communities on the Pacific Coast.

There is some **AA** here, during the winter, though it is a small group and mostly male. This is cheaper than many other places on the Pacific Coast. The best birding in Mexico is around here. If you are a **bohemian,** you could be happy here.

CONS

The beach is ugly. Additionally, it is populated with *jejénes,* also known as sand flies or no-see-ums. Local lore has it that Avon Skin-So-Soft is a good repellent, though scientific studies dispute this. These bugs can make an outing a miserable experience. Fortunately, they mostly come out at dusk. Because this is a really small town with few expatriates, you could easily get bored here. There is no culture. The tourists it attracts are mostly backpacker types. Communications are iffy. There is no Internet access. **Summers are very hot and humid. The Devil really does summer here.** There is not a lot of choice in places to live, and what there is, is basic. Forget luxury here. The RV parks are basic. Unless you really want to get away from it all, and are on a very tight budget, I can't imagine why you would want to live here.

IN-BETWEENS

Little English is spoken. If you are a bohemian or a birder, you will dig the place. If you are not, you will hate it. There are no in-betweens here. Love it or leave it.

✺ *Mazatlán, Sinaloa*

Altitude:	There is a hill.
Population:	250,000
Climate:	Mild most of the year. Can have hot days in summer.
Housing:	Moderate to expensive. From simple homes to gated communities and condos.
Ambiente:	Sun, surf, sand. Party-hearty.
Medical care:	Excellent.
Area code:	69

PROS

This small city is the **cheapest place to live** among Mexico's beach resorts. It is on the beach and the scenery is spectacular, from the islands in the middle of the bay to the cliffs along the Malecón, or waterfront drive. The city itself is interesting enough, with a feel of old Mexico—once you leave the Gold Zone, where all the hotels and tourist attractions are.

The fishing is among the best in Mexico, and Mazatlán is known as the billfish capital of the world. You can angle for marlin, sailfish, dorado and many more. The weather is great, winter and summer. The city has an international airport with direct flights from the United States. There is **strong English-speaking AA and Alanon** here year-round. There is adequate housing, in all price ranges. You could rent or buy anything from a simple Mexican house in a Mexican community to a condo on the beach to a luxurious villa in a gated community with a golf course. There are several RV parks, some with really nice facilities. If you want nightlife, there is plenty of it, mostly discos. There are bullfights. There is an English-language newspaper, the *Pacific Pearl,* P.O. Box 345, Mazatlán, Sin. The place is remarkably cultured, with the Angela Peralta Theater offering plays and concerts on a grand scale.

The medical care is first-rate, thanks to the Sharp Hospital, built in partnership with the hospital of the same name in San Diego, California. The equipment is new, the doctors and nurses are well-trained and it is the best-equipped hospital outside Mexico City. There is even plastic surgery done there, everything from breast implants or reductions to liposuction.

The **Carnaval,** though it doesn't rival that of Veracruz or New Orleans, is a growing event. The shrimp here are among the best in Mexico and you can buy them at the local market, or you can buy fresh fish from the fishermen on the beach. If you have culinary cravings, there are world-class chefs here. You can buy nearly any kind of consumer goods that you desire.

The Huichol Indians come to town occasionally and you could buy crafts directly from them. If you do, you will probably give them a better deal than they get from the local shops, some of which exploit them. One of the most interesting soft drinks in Mexico, Toni-Col, is sold here. It's rather like a vanilla cola. If the beach begins to bore you, you are only an hour's drive from the mountains. There, you could buy all the wooden furniture you need for your castle.

Communications are quite good and there is Internet access. You could conduct business from here, as the climate is very republican. It is virtually hurricane-proof. There is a very good aquarium.

There is an American consular officer here: Gerianne Nelson, Hotel Playa Mazatlán, Rodolfo Loyaza #207, Zona Dorada, 82100 Mazatlán, Sin., phone/fax: (69) 16-5889 (ask for the consular agent). There is also an American Legion Post.

CONS

If you do not get away from the Gold Zone, you will never experience the culture of the place. There are a lot of tourists. Much of the foreign community consists of time-share or real estate salespeople. After a while, you get a feeling that everyone is trying to make a buck from you. The **materialism and hedonism** of the place might affect you adversely after a while. During Carnaval and **spring break,** there are lots of rowdy teenage and college kids. Although I considered living here once, it is not very conducive to writing.

IN-BETWEENS

Lots of people here speak English. You will not be alone here, unless you want to be. Besides the foreign community, there is a constant stream of tourists who stay for a week to a month. **Gays and lesbians** will find friends here. You are not far from the United States by direct flights or by a nine-hour drive on the toll road.

❀ Alamos, Sonora

Altitude:	1,345 ft.
Population:	25,000
Climate:	Mild winters, hot summers.
Housing:	Limited. Varies from cheap to elegant.
Ambiente:	Laid-back, artistic, colonial.
Medical care:	Okay for a small town.
Area code:	642

PROS

This is **one of my favorite places,** a unique jewel in Mexico's crown. It's an old mining town that is rich in history and architecture. In fact, it has been declared a national monument by the Mexican government. As such, no new buildings can be erected in the old town, and all buildings must maintain their old colonial look.

Stepping into Alamos is like stepping back in time. The feeling here is truly **laid-back.** Although there is a respectable gringo community (for a town of its size), they are such an interesting lot that they don't overwhelm the town. Many of them speak Spanish and are involved in community projects. They have assimilated into the culture without eradicating it.

Besides the usual assortment of Americans who have chosen to live in Mexico, there are a few movie stars who prefer a place to get away from it all rather than the glamour and glitz of an Acapulco or Pto. Vallarta. I respect their desire for privacy so won't tell you who they are, but you'll no doubt run into them if you spend any time here.

The weather is not quite as hot as the surrounding desert and there are trees. In the winter, it has an **ideal dry climate.** The foreigners here are of all ages. The annual music festival attracts world-renowned musicians of all types. The social life can be quite active, so there's little chance you will feel lonely here. There are three **Spanish AA** groups; ask the bartender at Los Tesoros, seriously. The cost of living is a little bit higher than in a larger town, but you are close enough to the border to run up to Sam's for those things that Alamos doesn't offer.

Housing prices vary from relatively reasonable to very expensive. You should count on finding an old place, and if you want to save some money, get one outside the city limits. There are enough RV parks that you will have a choice of prices and facilities.

CONS

The weather is not suited to everyone's taste. Summer is still quite warm. It is a small community and you will know everyone and everyone's business in short order. There is a feeling of isolation to the town, and it is rather like Santa Fe, New Mexico, in that it could be too cute for some people's taste.

IN-BETWEENS

There is plenty of English spoken here. The foreign community is diverse— from artistic types who are barely making it to millionaires who live lavishly. Outside San Miguel de Allende and Oaxaca, you won't find a more interesting group. They are concerned about the community and seem to be a part of it. You won't find many Ugly Americans here. It would be a great setting in which to write a great novel or paint a masterpiece. Conducting business might be a challenge.

❂ *San Carlos, Sonora*

Altitude:	26 ft.
Population:	3,000
Climate:	Perfect winters. Warm-to-hot summers.
Housing:	Expensive. Scarce rentals. RV parks are often full.
Ambiente:	*Gringolandia.* Good fishing.
Medical care:	Surprisingly good for a small town. Hospitals nearby.
Area code:	622

PROS

This is a beautiful place, no doubt about it. That's why it is so popular with *norteamericanos.* Housing is sufficient, but on the **pricey** side. Besides houses, there are condominiums and several RV parks, which are often full. Some of the RV parks have plenty of amenities.

With so many Americans owning weekend houses or living here more or less full-time (though mainly in the winter), prices have skyrocketed.

There are plenty of restaurants, laundries and other amenities to keep you from feeling like you left everything behind to come here. Sonora is a progressive state and well-to-do. Many middle-class-and-above Mexicans also own property here. They flock here on the weekends, as do Arizonans.

The weather is pleasant, except in the summer, and even then it isn't too bad. The Gulf of California keeps things fairly moderate, though some will find it too hot. After all, you are on the edge of the desert. This keeps it from being too humid. The deep-sea **fishing** is excellent. There is a golf course. The whole town is rather amiable. Living here is pleasant. Communications are quite good. There is Internet access. Medical care is pretty good for such a small place and there is an ocean rescue squad who (with the help of volunteers) monitors the ship-to-shore radios. There is **English AA and Alanon** year-round. U.S. papers are available. Yachtsmen love the place and it has one of the largest marinas in Mexico. With its stark, dramatic setting, a nearby ocean (gulf really, but who's picky?) and generally pleasant *ambiente,* some people think of this as paradise. There is an international airport with flights back to Arizona.

CONS

It's hard to find anything bad to say about San Carlos. It is close enough to the United States to be accessible and far enough into Mexico to be worth the trip. It is a small town, though, and this could get to some people. The foreign community dominates the town, so English is widely spoken. You could live here and never learn a lick of Spanish. It is costly, and even the RV parks are higher than in other places. If you are on a **tight budget, you might have to really hunt for somewhere to live.**

IN-BETWEENS

You could isolate yourself and write a novel, or get involved with the large gringo community. There are more expatriates nearer to sixty than forty. You could conduct a business here, even one in Arizona, if you telecommuted; it's only a 250-mile drive on a beautiful four-lane toll road. The movie *Catch-22* was shot here. There is a Club Med at the old location, but they don't bother anybody. English is commonly spoken.

Guaymas, Sonora

Altitude:	26 ft.
Population:	150,000
Climate:	Hot summers, mild winters.
Housing:	Less expensive than San Carlos. More choices.
Ambiente:	Not much. A commercial port city.
Medical care:	Adequate.
Area code:	622

PROS

Guaymas is a seaport and naval station. This makes it a fair-sized town with some of the amenities that you'd find in a larger city. Because it is more of a Mexican community than San Carlos, **housing costs are lower.** There is more available and at a cheaper price. Of course, you don't have the ocean views, but you don't have to pay for them. There is a hospital. There are RV parks and one of them is quite nice; the rest are good enough. If you cannot afford to live in San Carlos, you might consider Guaymas.

CONS

It is not very pretty. There is almost no beach. You will hear a lot more Spanish than English.

IN-BETWEENS

You get more of a feel of living in a Mexican community. If you make the effort, you can learn more about Mexican society by living here. Although there are some discos, that's about the extent of the nightlife. You probably will not be intellectually stimulated here.

Kino Bay (Bahía Kino), Sonora

Altitude:	Not much.
Population:	1,500

Climate:	Mild winters, hot summers.
Housing:	Inexpensive but limited availability.
Ambiente:	Quiet. Good fishing. Small-town.
Medical care:	Limited.
Area code:	624

108

PROS

Kino Bay is a **small fishing community** on the Gulf of California, just seventy three miles west of the capital of Hermosillo. It is the closest seaside village to the Arizona border, except for Pto. Peñasco, farther north and west. It is quiet and **laid-back,** except on weekends. Housing is reasonable, less than San Carlos. There are several RV parks.

The beach is beautiful, but the surrounding desert is barren. Winters are comfortable. There is great seafood and the fishing is good. The Seri Indians have a store in Old Kino where you can buy their handiwork, most notably carvings of ironwood. If you are adventurous, you can drive (with a four-wheel vehicle) to some of their villages north of town and buy directly from them. There is **English AA and Alanon** here. Many more meetings are held in the winter than in the summer due to the lack of gringos living there in the summer. Once you are here, you can do most of your getting around on foot.

CONS

This is a really small community, especially in summer, for good reason. It is **beastly hot in the summer.** There is little to do. On weekends it fills up with wealthy people from Hermosillo. The adults are fine people, but the teenagers, *los juniors,* like to run their ATVs up and down the beach, spoiling the tranquillity. Although this activity is technically illegal, no local cop in his right mind would take one to task for it. You could get bored here. Medical care is limited, but you are not that far from Hermosillo, a modern city with hospitals. You are only a few hours from the Arizona border. In order to buy anything except the basics, you'll have to run up to Hermosillo. There aren't a lot of rentals.

IN-BETWEENS

Many people here speak English. It is a really quiet place. The crowd in the summer is mostly RVers and they tend to be older. Communications are adequate, but not abundant. Conducting business, unless it is one based in Arizona, would be a challenge.

⊗ *Pto. Peñasco, Sonora*

Altitude:	Sea level.
Population:	20,000
Climate:	Mild winters, hot summers.
Housing:	Real estate is very expensive.
Ambiente:	Small fishing port with lots and lots of Americans and weekend visitors from Arizona. English is widely spoken.
Medical care:	Adequate. There is a hospital, but for major care, most people go back to Arizona.
Area code:	638

PROS

This is the closest beach to Arizona and a lot of Zonies (Arizonans) live here. On weekends, it is full of visitors. They are a well-behaved bunch, for the most part, so the town does not lose its charm when they arrive. You will be able to get along here without speaking Spanish if that is what you want to do.

The views of the bay and the beaches are dramatic. The atmosphere is laid-back and still very Mexican. Prices are on the upswing, but it is still less expensive than the Baja. There is a development called La Choya where less expensive houses can be found. There are condos, houses and apartments for rent, as well as RV spaces. Although I would not type this as a budgeteer's haven, you could find a place here without being a millionaire. In fact, I know people who live here on about $600 a month. Las Conchas is a pricey, exclusive community with guards and security patrols, etc. You could spend $150,000–$250,000 for the privilege of living here.

The seafood is great, but the fishing has gone downhill from its glory days. The locals have a wonderfully acceptant attitude toward the gringos. Because it is a small town, you will soon know everyone. There is **English**

AA and even an English-language monthly newspaper, the *Rocky Point Times,* P.O. Box 887, Lukeville, AZ 85341. Subscriptions are $30 for twelve issues. It is well written and many people subscribe to it back home to keep up with the community.

CONS

Some may find the **preponderance of Americans** to be exactly what they wanted to get away from. The smallness of the community means that you will know most everyone's business before too long. The cost of living can be expensive. Summers are hot.

IN-BETWEENS

You don't even need a tourist permit or car permit to come here. You are close enough to the United States to bring down anything you need. Customs is sometimes lenient, sometimes not. I can't guarantee that you will be able to bring everything you want without paying some duty, but there seems to be no dearth of material possessions in the homes of the foreigners.

Baja California

There are actually **two states** that make up the Baja Peninsula—Baja California Norte and Baja California Sur. **Baja is very different from mainland Mexico.** The two states operated as free territories until fairly recently. Due to their physical isolation from the rest of the country and the proximity of California, they have more in common with California than with Mexico City in many ways. Most of the foreign residents of the Baja are

Baja is an entirely different kettle of fish than mainland Mexico. Those who love it, love it passionately. Those who dislike it are equally passionate. It is not for everyone.

Californians. Although Baja is still Mexico, it is more progressive than many mainland states in general and more English is spoken.

Baja is a land of **stark contrasts and great natural beauty.** Nature lovers adore it. There are still some very isolated spots on Baja where four-wheel-drive vehicles are a necessity. The main highway, which runs north–south from the border at Tijuana to Cabo San Lucas, is a good, paved road. Near the population centers it is four-lane. In the middle, it is a two-lane road, easily driven by all but the new, wider-body RVs.

The foreigners who have settled here are a mixed breed. There are those in Los Cabos (which means both Cabo San Lucas and San José del Cabo) who have turned the area into a little California. There are those around San Felipe and south of there who are old-style desert rats who wanted to get away from their countrymen. In between there are people who fit neither category and chose Baja as a resting place because they love the land and the people. Every Baja town is different and could suit someone.

San Felipe, Baja California

Altitude:	If you stand on top of a building.
Population:	6,100
Climate:	Hot, hot, hot summers. Mild winters.
Housing:	Lots of availability, but prices are high because of all the Americans here.
Ambiente:	Strange mix of California/Arizona/Mexico. Lots of U.S. influence.
Medical care:	Adequate.
Area code:	657

PROS

It is close to the U.S. border, only 118 miles. Living here can be dirt (sand, really) cheap in RV parks that are little more than spots on the sand without hookups, or expensive in classy condos or luxury houses. There are first-class RV parks with clubhouses and Jacuzzis. They are as expensive as any in the United States. The town is small and pleasant. It was a fishing community, but today tourism is the main industry. There are plenty of hotels and restaurants in all price ranges except rock-bottom. **Everything here is expensive,** by mainland Mexico standards, but cheap for Baja.

There is plenty of English spoken. The scenery is a stark desert. The Gulf of California is dramatic. There are hills in town that have serpentine streets and lots of houses. The winters are pleasant. There is **English AA and Alanon** here, and women-only meetings, which is great if you live here, but a real drag if you are a tourist. There is a **hot spring** nearby, in Puertocitos, and another on private land north of town. The fishing is not as good as it used to be because of the degradation of the Gulf of California, which has been declared an ecological protection zone, about ten years too late. Communications are excellent.

CONS

The economy is **dollar-based,** so you do not benefit from a good exchange rate. On weekends the place is full, often with rowdy people of all ages who come down to party. Then you will see more Americans than Mexicans. It is

hotter than Hades in the summer. For me, it is too much like California (and I am a recovering Californian and like California and Californians) and not enough like Mexico.

IN-BETWEENS

If you just want to get to warm winters and don't mind a lot of Americans and can put up with the weekenders, this could be the place for you. It can be cheap, if you are willing to live basically in an RV.

❂ *Puertocitos and Beyond*

Altitude:	If you stand on top of a building.
Population:	6,100
Climate:	Hot, hot, hot summers. Mild winters.
Housing:	Lots of availability, but prices are high because of all the Americans here.
Ambiente:	Haven for "don't tread on me" escapees from civilization.
Medical care:	Primitive.
Area code:	657

PROS

The road is paved south to Puertocitos and a little beyond. **Puertocitos has a hot spring,** though it didn't impress me. My friend Carl Franz, author of *The People's Guide to Mexico* (required reading for anyone who wants to understand the Mexican culture), asked me not to reveal it. I intended to keep my promise, but when I got there, it was so obviously well known by everyone in San Felipe, and **such a disappointment** to me, that I saw no harm in telling the world about it. It is also in some guidebooks.

There are scads of Americans living here, on the hills overlooking the Gulf. They are a different lot than in San Felipe—people who wanted to get away from development. It looks a little like an old version of Sausalito, California, perhaps around the time of Jack Kerouac.

As you drive south, you will find RVs and desert rats parked on isolated beaches. For those who want nothing more than the isolation of being in a magnificent natural setting, these little *campos* could be for you. If you make it all the way to **Bahia San Luis Gonzaga** (four-wheel drive recommended), you will find a tight-knit community of people who really wanted to get away from it all. There's not much to the town and "the" street is also a landing strip. Most of the residents are foreigners. If you are a self-sufficient type and a nature lover, you will love this area. It is still unspoiled (except for the horde of gringos who live here) and truly stupendous in its beauty.

114

CONS

If you are not a self-sufficient type and a nature lover, you will go out of your skull here. You've got to pack everything in, and what you have to buy is expensive. Communications are almost nonexistent.

IN-BETWEENS

There aren't any. You love it or hate it.

❂ *Mulegé, Baja California Sur*

Altitude:	Not much.
Population:	6,100
Climate:	Mild winters. Hot, humid summers.
Housing:	Reasonable for the Baja. Not a lot of choices.
Ambiente:	Laid-back, quiet.
Medical care:	Adequate for a small town. For major emergencies, plan on being airlifted.
Area code:	115

PROS

If I were going to live in Baja, this would be the place. It is an **oasis** (literally) in the desert, with a river, trees and even orchards. It has a quiet, laid-back feel to it, and the Mexicans outnumber the gringos. There isn't a lot to do, and that is one of its attractions. There are some restaurants and hotels with some entertainment, but it ain't the Great White Way.

Mulegé has the fame of once having had a prison where the inmates were on the honor system. They could visit town during the day, but had to return to incarceration at night. If one strayed, they were all punished. It worked rather well. There are RV parks and modest houses. **Housing is not as expensive** as other places in the Baja, and not as plentiful. There was an **English AA** group here, but I don't know if they are still there. Let me know.

Scuba diving is very good in the late summer and fall (August–November). Fishing is great, with yellowtail, rooster fish and pargo close to shore near the estuary, and in the summer offshore you can catch dorado, billfish and yellowfin.

CONS

The **quiet, simple lifestyle** could get to you after a while. It is not for everyone. Manufactured goods are expensive. Communications are iffy.

IN-BETWEENS

It's a love-it-or-leave-it place. Many people settle here "for the rest of their lives" and leave in a few years.

⊛ *Loreto, Baja California Sur*

Altitude:	Not much.
Population:	Approximately 6,000
Climate:	Hot, hot, hot summers. Mild winters.
Housing:	Lots of condos and time-shares. Pricey.
Ambiente:	Upscale, planned development.
Medical care:	Adequate.
Area code:	113

PROS

This is a **beautiful** place. Developers have been trying to promote it for years, but it has never quite caught on. There are plans for a gringo retirement community with all the amenities. I cannot say whether it is a good deal or a bad deal, as I have not seen it. Costs are par for the Baja, but less than in Los Cabos. Windsurfing is good. The climate is excellent in the winter. Fishing is often very good, with sailfish, dorado, snapper, tuna and marlin waiting for you in the summer. Winter favors yellowtail and sierra. There is an excellent RV park in Pto. Escondido, about thirty miles south.

CONS

I sometimes wonder if the place is star-crossed. There are always grand projects for it, but they never quite jell. One reason may be that the **summer is ungodly hot**. Very few foreigners want to stay here in the summer.

IN-BETWEENS

There is always the possibility that the development plans for the area will take off and it will turn into another Cabo.

◉ *La Paz, Baja California Sur*

Altitude:	Sea level.
Population:	300,000
Climate:	Moderately hot summers (cooler than Loreto) and mild winters.
Housing:	Plentiful in all price ranges.
Ambiente:	Cultured, laid-back. Old-style Baja.
Medical care:	Excellent.
Area code:	112

PROS

I have always liked the town. It is large enough to offer many services and small enough to have a real sense of community. There is an **interesting mix** of foreigners who live or visit here and they generally have good attitudes. The constant influx of yachtsmen gives it a truly international flavor, besides providing great views in the bay. The attitude of the residents is cordial and typifies all that is good about the Baja. Live-and-let-live and genuine friendliness seem to permeate the atmosphere. For example, there are numerous four-way stops. I have never seen anyone go out of turn or honk his horn. There are RV parks and housing that ranges from very expensive to reasonable. The weather is beautiful, though warm in the summer. The fishing is great, with yellowtail

> *La Paz means "the peace" and you will find just that here. It attracts a completely different crowd than Cabo.*

caught from January to March and marlin, pargo, rooster fish, sierra and my favorite, pompano, usually caught from April to November. There is now Internet access.

Housing is **much less expensive than Cabo** and has a lot **more character.** For those who like nightlife, there is enough variety here to satisfy most everyone, though it does not have the glitz and glamour of Cabo. Scuba diving is excellent.

CONS

I really can't think of any.

IN-BETWEENS

In the winter there are bullfights. **Carnaval** is a big deal here and some say it is better than Mazatlán's. Another big event is the **Fiesta de la Fundación de la Ciudad de la Paz,** held May 3.

✸ *Cabo San Lucas, Baja California Sur*

Altitude:	96 ft.
Population:	45,000 (combined for Cabo and San José)
Climate:	Moderately hot summers (cooler than Loreto) and mild winters.
Housing:	Plentiful in all price ranges.
Ambiente:	Similar to being in southern California. English is widely spoken. Many foreigners, time-share salesmen. Party-hearty crowd.
Medical care:	Excellent.
Area code:	114

PROS

This is the end of the Baja, both literally and figuratively. It is the **most developed** of the towns in the southern Baja and has the most to offer. The sea and the beaches are dramatic and the sunsets are breathtaking. In fact, watching the sunsets is a favorite activity. There are several RV parks, condominiums, houses and apartments. They are all **expensive,** roughly on par with southern California. One resident told me that her two-bedroom trailer cost $160,000 plus $350 a month for her space.

There are less expensive RV parks (about $200 a month), but the one above is typical of the really nice ones. Houses can easily run a quarter of a million dollars, although I saw ads for two-bedroom houses for around $100,000. Like anywhere else, the key is location, location, location. Only recently has there been Internet access and it is more expensive than on the mainland—about $35–$40 for twenty hours.

There are lots of Californians here, particularly on weekends. Many have condos or time-shares here. Many live here for extended periods of time. You will hear a lot of English and you don't really need to speak Spanish to get along quite well here. There is **English AA** and **Alanon,** with regular meetings. The fishing is superior. It is known as the marlin capital of the world and there are also sailfish and swordfish. Both the blue and the black marlin are caught here. Catch-and-release has caught on here and you are allowed only one billfish per boat. Scuba diving is very good. Snorkeling is also good.

You can get English-language newspapers daily. Cabo has a lot to offer those who appreciate its charms. Locals are very proud of their world-class golf courses—six of them, between Cabo and San José. There is an American consular agent: Robin Hann, Blvd. Marian y Pedregal, Local 3, Zona Centro, phone/fax: (114) 3-3566. There is a dandy English-language newspaper, the *Gringo Gazette,* 532 E. 4th St., Long Beach, CA 90802; 310-436-3433, fax: 310-436-5080. Subscriptions are $46 for one year (twenty-six issues) and $24.50 for six months (thirteen issues).

CONS

Among the attractions of the place is the extensive nightlife. The world-famous discos feature world-famous bands and can be very loud. The downtown area is too **noisy** at night for me to sleep. On weekends, another of the charms is the thousands of foreigners who fly down, many of whom are there to party. It is **expensive** as can be. You sometimes get the feeling that everyone wants something from you, from the time-share hustlers to the vendors. The charm of this formerly isolated oasis has been eradicated by the Americanization of it.

IN-BETWEENS

You either love it or hate it.

❋ *San José del Cabo, Baja California Sur*

Altitude:	96 ft.
Population:	39,000
Climate:	Moderately hot summers (cooler than Loreto) and mild winters.
Housing:	Plentiful in all price ranges.
Ambiente:	More relaxed and less glitzy than Cabo.
Medical care:	Excellent.
Area code:	114

This is just northeast of Cabo San Lucas and is much less Americanized. **It has more charm,** a more Mexican atmosphere and is **less expensive.** It has plenty of restaurants and there are RV parks between the two. There is plenty of housing, in all varieties, for about half the cost of Cabo. It is possible to rent an apartment here for around $400 a month. The nightlife is a lot more subdued. If I had to live in either, I would choose San José.

The Gulf Coast

This is an area that hasn't gotten a lot of attention as a part of the country to live in. This, in itself, is an attraction to many. There are some desirable locations close to the U.S. border—a day's drive. The beaches are quite nice and varied—undeveloped expanses of white sand in the North and tropical, palm tree–lined ones in the South. There are not a lot of foreign residents, so those of you who are looking for a community of *paisanos* had best look inland. Those who are looking for a place where they can mingle with the locals will love it.

The roads are often bad, the weather can be less than perfect, with hurricanes in the summer and occasional cold fronts (where the temperature might drop to 40 degrees Fahrenheit) for a few days. It is close to the U.S. border. There are no really good medical facilities outside Veracruz.

The atmosphere is **laid-back.** The people are really friendly. The seafood is excellent.

⊛ El Paraiso, Tam.

Altitude:	45 ft.
Population:	6,100
Climate:	Very hot summers and mild winters.
Housing:	Limited.
Ambiente:	Isolated, for nature lovers.
Medical care:	Nonexistent.
Area code:	12

PROS

This is **one of my favorite places** in Mexico. Only five hours from either McAllen or Brownsville, Texas, it could be a **great alternative to the Rio**

Grande Valley of Texas, where thousands of Winter Texans (snowbirds) flock every year. Right now, it is not set up for a retirement community, but the owner, Francisco Haces, has big plans. He intends to build an exclusive subdivision for retirees in a remote, ecological paradise.

The plan is to have small houses and to offer complete pampering—from catered meals with a dietary consultant on the premises, to an ecological golf course, to birding trips and scads of activities. I thought that the words "ecological" and "golf course" went together about as well as "army" and "intelligence," but Francisco explained that there is sufficient rainfall and morning dew there to allow him to build a course without having to waste water keeping it up. Okay. If he is able to pull it off, this will be a great place to winter. I have high hopes for his venture, but one never knows. It is at least a year and maybe two from fruition.

To check on the progress of this venture, call 1-800-321-5605. For pictures of the area, go to www.mexicomike.com/el_paraiso.htm. You can also make reservations to go down to check the place out at this number. Right now, Francisco has a unique resort that has been in operation for several years. Fishing is great for bass, snook and tarpon in the river and trout, redfish, snapper, skipjack, pompano and flounder in the Gulf. The beach is unspoiled and the atmosphere is tranquil.

CONS
This is really isolated. Once you are there, you are there. It is ideal for those who want to get away from it all right now. Once Francisco gets his retirement community going, there will be activities and social life, but it will be a small community.

IN-BETWEENS
You will either love it or hate it.

A Story about El Paraiso (the resort)
Paradise is only a few hours away. Perhaps I should rephrase that. For some, paradise would be a packed disco on a Cancún Saturday night and a pocket full of money and gold cards. For those people, El Paraiso Resort in nearby Tamaulipas will not do.

If your idea of paradise is a quiet, comfortable, romantic place, set in a unique river landscape with respect for the ecology, miles of absolutely deserted beaches and **thousands of birds (including wild parrots that fly over your room twice a day)**, then this might be your sort of retreat.

El Paraiso Resort is near Barra del Tordo, Tamaulipas, which is only **five hours south** of the Texas/Mexico border at McAllen or Brownsville. It can be a romantic getaway, a naturalist's dream vacation, the spot for your next spiritual retreat or a good location for your company's board meeting or small convention. If you are a fisherman, it is very close to heaven.

El Paraiso is an **ecological cornucopia.** Francisco Haces realized that a few years ago and started billing his lodge as an ecotourism place. To be sure, you can still fish in the river in front of the lodge, or in the Gulf of Mexico only minutes away, but catch-and-release is encouraged. I have gotten to know Francisco as a friend over the years and he (like a lot of us) has gone through a transformation in the past few years.

This is a **quiet, romantic** getaway spot. Imagine being ferried to your weekend hideaway in a motorboat. Once you are there, the atmosphere, particularly at night, is that of being on a remote tropical paradise. The *cabañas* and grounds are illuminated with a soft, yellow light.

The lodge is set high on a bluff overlooking the river. On the way to your room, you'll pass a sparkling swimming pool and several neatly furnished individual *cabañas* with ornamental thatched roofs, air-conditioning and tiled bathrooms. There's a family room where meals are served and guests can gather to chat. To me the advantage of a place like this over a high-rise resort is that you can socialize. Kiko will be around to greet you and make sure that your stay is a pleasant one.

Naturalists will love the fact that they can see dozens of sea and shore birds, including osprey, hawks, egrets, eagles, cranes and parrots. In the winter, ducks abound. Fish, including tarpon, snook and bass, jump in the river and its estuaries.

During the day, you can take advantage of boat rides down lagoons to catch glimpses of dozens of species of birds or to explore the estuaries. Farther down the river is the Gulf of Mexico, with miles and miles of truly deserted white-sand beaches. Imagine you and your sweetie frolicking on fine white sand with miles of pounding surf and driftwood your only companions. The endangered Kemp's Ridley sea turtles use the area to nest, up the coast a ways.

Nearby, back toward the highway, is the deepest hole in the earth (over 1,000 feet deep), a *cenote,* or natural well. It is the deepest on earth—yes, deeper than the ones in the Yucatán. Two divers from the University of Texas discovered its bottom, but one died of the bends on the way up. The water is as clear and turquoise as any *cenote* I have seen in the Yucatán. There is also a sulfur hot spring and a cave in the neighborhood. The survivor returned recently to finish his exploration.

To get there from McAllen or Brownsville, drive down Hwy. 97 or 101 to Hwy. 180 and keep going south toward Tampico. At **Aldama,** take a left toward the Gulf of Mexico and drive forty-one kilometers. The scenery changes dramatically from the flatland you've just traversed to gentle rolling hills. Ignore the Coca-Cola sign at kilometer 37. At kilometer 41, you'll see a Coca-Cola sign that reads "El Paraiso." Turn left again and go through a pasture (yes, you can drive it in the family sedan, unless it has rained recently). Watch that cow! The parking lot is a nice cleared field shaded by hundred-year-old trees. There's twenty-four-hour security.

You can also fly to Tampico. Kiko can arrange to meet you at the airport and take you to El Paraiso. Rates are reasonable, approximately $95 per person, per day, which includes three excellent meals daily. You really have to make a reservation, so call 1-800-321-4622. There are special rates for groups. Tell Francisco that "Mexico" Mike sent you and then be ready to duck.

◉ Tecolutla, Veracruz

Altitude:	Sea level.
Population:	2,000
Climate:	Hot summers and mild winters. During the rainy (and hurricane) season (May–Sept.) severe storms.
Housing:	Limited.
Ambiente:	Mexico of yesteryear. Small fishing village, few foreigners.
Medical care:	Barely adequate.
Area code:	784

PROS
Tecolutla is the largest town in this collection of small communities along the Gulf of Mexico between Tecolutla and Cardel, just north of Veracruz.

> *Excellent seafood, good fishing and a French influence make up this almost foreigner-less town on the Gulf of Mexico.*

Tecoluta is on the beach and has almost white- (there's a tinge of volcanic gray to it) sand beaches with palm trees almost to the water's edge. The seafood is excellent and the fishing very good. There is a **French influence**, as it was here that many of the deserters from the French army hid out after their rout at Puebla. Although the food is not really French, it has a basis in French cuisine so that it is unique in Mexico. You won't meet any French-speakers here, but there is French blood in the veins of many of the residents. Some of them have blue eyes!

Housing is inexpensive, if hard to come by. There are some developments along the beach between Casitas and Nautla, with condos and homes, but Tecolutla itself has only modest homes with a few rentals. For those drawn to these laid-back communities, it will be worth the effort to find an abode here. The people are friendly, the weather is fine during the winter (except for those few times when a norther blows in and the temperature drops to the forties) and everything is reasonably priced. There are many RV parks, but they do not offer a lot of services. If you are looking for a place to get away from it all, this is it.

CONS

This is really off the beaten track. There will be **little English** spoken. The very smallness of the communities may get to you after a while. There is no English AA, but there are several Spanish-speaking groups. There are few foreigners, except a few RVers during the winter. Medical care is barely adequate, though there is a good doctor in Casitas, a friend of mine, who has a traveling clinic and goes into the smaller communities to help those less fortunate than himself. If you feel generous (or sick), look up Dr. Silvero Herrera, phone: (232) 5-0860 or 5-0807, ext. 153 or 113. For serious emergencies, you'll have to go to Veracruz, or back to the States.

IN-BETWEENS

The scenery is tropical. You could settle here and write or paint to your heart's content. If you are self-sufficient, or if your budget is slim, this could be your place. If isolation doesn't appeal to you, then you had better look elsewhere.

✵ *Veracruz, Veracruz*

Altitude:	Sea level.
Population:	550,000
Climate:	Hot summers and mild winters.
Housing:	Housing prices have gone down over the last several years.
Ambiente:	Sultry, sophisticated, a lot like New Orleans with music, dancing and parades and Mardi Gras (Carnaval). Few foreigners and not much English spoken.
Medical care:	There is a hospital that gives good care. Plenty of doctors and specialists.
Area code:	29

PROS

This is a **lively** place. There is always **music** in the square, from **marimba** bands to navy band concerts. The *danzon* is a big weekly street dance. The **seafood is the best in Mexico**. It is gay-friendly and there are gay clubs that specialize in transvestite shows. The weather is generally warm in the winter, except for those few times when a *norteño* makes it this far south and drops the temperatures to the upper forties. These spells last only a day or two and then warm weather returns.

Housing is reasonable and varies from condominiums to apartments to houses. Because this is Mexico's most important port, it has the flavor of a world-class seaport. The **Carnaval** is the best in Mexico and some prefer it to the one in New Orleans.

There is a strong **Lebanese** community with social clubs and restaurants. Medical care is good and Mexico City is only a few hours away. There is no organized English AA, though there is sometimes a loner here. There are several Spanish-speaking groups that are quite friendly. There is an American consular agent here: Edwin Culp, Víctimas del 25 de Junio #388, 91700 Veracruz, Ver., phone: (29) 31-5821, fax: (29) 31-6941.

CONS

There is no organized foreign community and retirees won't find many *paisanos* to socialize with. The weather is **humid** all the time. The **beach is** not very pretty, being a volcanic gray sand. There is one RV park, but it is no more than a place to park (on the beach, though) with some limited electricity and no dump station. It is not a very quiet city. In fact, its very character precludes that, unless you are in one of the elegant suburbs. The traffic is bad.

IN-BETWEENS

This is a place for people who like a lot of excitement. The atmosphere is **sultry and decadent.** For someone who wants to spend some lively time in an exciting Mexican cosmopolitan community, it could be just the ticket. For someone who wants to retire, it might be a little too intense. It is quite **gay-friendly** and you will find plenty of company here; there are transvestite clubs with floor shows. If you like New Orleans, you will like Veracruz, as the atmosphere is very similar.

General Information

AA and Other 12 Step Programs

GENERAL ADVICE ON STAYING SOBER IN MEXICO—
THE SPECIAL PITFALLS

You'll find AA throughout Mexico, even in small towns. NA has a sizable presence in the larger towns. Alanon is almost everywhere. OA, SALA and other programs are less likely to be encountered outside major cities. AA is very visible. I have noted where there are meetings in many cases, but like in the States, they move or change.

Look for the AA symbol inside a triangle and a circle, usually on a blue background jutting out from buildings. Meetings are usually at 8 or 8:30 P.M. in Spanish. **Even if you don't speak Spanish, you will be welcome** and often asked to speak. This is true all over the world. I have been to meetings in Cuba, Europe and England (where they speak a foreign language, vaguely similar to English) and have always been welcome. Come to think of it, these are the only places where I can count on being welcome. Go ahead. It will do you good. Meetings last an hour and a half and there are often refreshments, and birthdays are celebrated like they are in the States, except you might get tamales instead of cake, or both. Have a ball.

You don't have to leave your program behind when you cross the border. There is more to enjoy in Mexico than the tequila. AA is very strong in Mexico, and they are not at all anonymous about it. Most of the towns with a sizable gringo population will have English-speaking meetings. If not—find a loner, go to a Spanish-speaking meeting or start your own group.

You'll be pleasantly surprised to find English-speaking meetings in most towns with a large gringo presence. Just in case you forgot your International Directory, I have included a list of all the ones I know about, arranged by geographic sections of the country (see page 130).

Just like in the United States, the locations change, so if a meeting is no longer where I said it was, you have two courses of action (aside from giving up and giving in). Believe me, looking for a meeting is often a better choice than going back to your hotel where the "Chug-tequila-till-you-barf" contest is going on. The first option is to check the local English-language newspaper if there is one. The second option is to find a Spanish meeting and ask.

One night I was in San Miguel de Allende and the English-language meeting had moved. I was ready to get drunk as my companion and was crestfallen. I wandered the late-night streets of town, bemoaning my fate. For some reason I looked up and I saw the familiar triangle in a circle. I was in front of a Mexican AA club. The meeting was over, but the guys there could see that I was in trouble. Six of us piled into a Volkswagen and went roaring down the midnight streets.

There I was, in a car of strangers who spoke no English (my Spanish was poor then), going to God knew where. A bar full of happy (?) Americans seemed a lot more inviting. Oh, well. They took me to a midnight meeting. Although I didn't understand a word they said, I felt the companionship and caring that is universal. Those guys saved my life. So, if a meeting has moved since I wrote this, don't use that as an excuse to get drunk. Get off the pity pot and find a meeting. Then let me know about any changes.

For Alanon and NA, etc., these places will be able to direct you as well, though **NA is not as "popular."** You'll be welcome at an AA meeting. There are **two different types of AA** in Mexico. One is "Grupo de Viente Cuatro Horas" (24-hour group). These are more like institutional settings and the message here is hard core, "put-the-plug-in-the-jug"-type.

The other is more like what you are used to. Be prepared for $1^1/_2$-hour-long meetings, with long orations and lots of slang. They are very emotional. You will be asked to say something. Do your best and take care of yourself. If **the above fails and you can't find a meeting, try putting up signs in your hotel and others about a meeting in your room. Then stay there.**

While we are on the subject of drinking, forget the myth that some folks will tell you that it is a shooting offense to refuse a drink offered by a

Mexican. You can refuse to do anything you want if you do it politely. Many times Mexicans are only offering to share something with you because they are being polite. They would never expect you to do something that would cause you harm. If you simply say, *"No gracias, no bebo cerveza (tequila, ron,* etc., or simply *alcohól), pero quisiera un refresco,"* you'll probably get a soft drink instead and no one will be offended.

129

If the guy insists that you have a drink with him, be as polite as possible, and just as insistent. Plead illness, medication or whatever you are comfortable with. Saying *"soy alérgico a alcohól"* sometimes does the trick, but saying you are an alcoholic may elicit a blank stare. *If all else fails, get up and walk away.* Offending a drunk does not rank as a punishable offense in any country, and you have to remember what's really important.

Be especially careful ordering tonic water or *agua quina* in bars or restaurants. You'll often end up with gin and tonic, because the waiter thought you didn't speak Spanish well enough. Stick with *agua mineral* or Coke or 7-Up, or a local soft drink. There are some great local ones. Toni-Col on the West Coast, especially near Mazatlán, is one of the best. It does have caffeine, so if you are trying to avoid that, you'd best avoid Toni-Col, but darn, it is good. It's rather like a vanilla Coke. Of course, I have heard of drinkers who ordered J&B and soda and got Jim Beam and Coke.

When asking if a dish has alcohol in it, be sure to ask if it has wine too. For some reason, **wine is not considered alcohol by waiters.** Often they will say, "Oh, no, there is no alcohol, only a little wine." I subscribe to the school that it does not cook out. Even if you don't believe that to be true at home, **believe it in Mexico. Trust me.**

Coffees with fancy names like "Sexy, Spanish, German or Lithuanian" (just kidding about the last one) are suspect. If the price is more than plain coffee *(Americano or negro or cafe con leche),* then it is a booze drink. It's rare, but I have had Amaretto poured over *flan,* the great dessert. Always use the sniff test before eating anything with a sauce on it. If you accidentally imbibe something with booze, spit it out and don't worry about it. It happens to the best. Just don't take a second swig or taste, and forget about it.

If you have an AA medallion or ring and wear it, you'll be surprised at the people you'll meet. If we ever meet in person, I'll tell you a story that was related to me about that.

That's all the sobriety wisdom I have and I hope it helps at least one person. The main thing to remember is that **you are not alone even in**

Mexico and that you can still have a great trip and not lose your program. Your help in getting new information is appreciated—you know how these groups move around. **Spanish for "meeting" is *reunión* or *sesión*.** The phone numbers below were either provided by the contact person or came from newspapers, so I'm not breaking anyone's anonymity.

MEETING LOCATIONS AND SCHEDULES

Baja

Cabo San Lucas
Hotel Hacienda, on the veranda. Sun., Mon., Wed., Fri. 7 P.M.

Ensenada Area—Punta Banda
AA meetings have changed a lot. Men's AA, Catholic Church, La Jolla Beach, Mon. 10 A.M.; Women's 12 Step, Train Room, Casa de Riker, La Jolla Beach, Mon. 10 A.M.; Catholic Church, La Jolla Beach, Tues. 8 A.M.; Catholic Church, La Jolla Beach, Thurs. 8 A.M.; "Going to Any Length" AA, Train Room, Casa de Riker, La Jolla Beach, Sat. 8 A.M.

La Paz
"Group Esperanza" AA, daily 9–10 A.M. Calle Madero between Navarro and Encinas. Contact Casa Blanca Trailer Park.

Maneadero, B.C.
Cultural Social Salón (on Hwy. 1), 10.6 miles south of Ensenada at junction. with paved road to Bufadora, Sun. 10 A.M. Ask for Albert.

Mulegé
One block east of Canada store, Fri. 3 P.M.

Rosarito Beach, B.C.
El Grupo Gringo on 72 Calle Palma up the street from Rosarito Beach Hotel, Sun., Mon. 10 A.M. Book study Tues. 7 P.M., Wed. 6 P.M., Thurs. 10 A.M. Step Study Fri. 7 P.M., Sat. 3 P.M.

San Felipe, B.C.
There is a meeting hall on the south end of the highway through town, on

the left by a car wash, about halfway through town. Some meetings are women-only, so check the schedule on the front before barging in.

Todos los Santos, B.C.
There are a couple of loners here. Ask around.

West Coast

Acapulco
English-speaking group meets at Horacio Nelson #250. Nelson runs from the Wal-Mart store to the church behind Baby O's disco. #250 is about halfway down the street. Turn left (away from the water), off the *Costera* at the intersection with Oceanic 2000 on beach side and with 100% Natural and Banca Confía across the street on corners. Go one block to Calle Horacio Nelson, and turn right. AA Club is about midblock at #250 on beach side of street across from Splash Car Wash. Wed., Fri. 5 P.M. In the winter there are four or five meetings a week. There are Spanish-speaking meetings at the same locations every day 6:30–8 P.M.

Kino Bay, Son.
Club Deportivo, Wed., Sat. 7 P.M. at El Saguaro trailer park rec room. Call Chuck or Gloria. Phone: (624) 2-0141.

Manzanillo, Col.
On the beach in front of Willy's Restaurant, Wed. 10 A.M.

Mazatlán, Sin.
333 Cameron Sabalo #6 (across from the Guadalajara Grill) in the Zona Dorada. This is a shopping center next to Las Palmas Trailer Park. Mon., Wed., Fri. 6:30–7:30 P.M., Nov.–Mar. on Sun. 10–11 A.M. Contact Barbara R., phone: 16-1568, or Ed L., phone: 14-0174. Same location has Spanish meetings Mon.–Fri. 8–9:30 P.M., and Wed., Thurs., Fri. 8:30–10 A.M.

Pto. Vallarta, Jal.
Meets at Edificio Cine Bahia (in older section of town, across the Río Cuale at 181 Insurgentes, near Madero), 2nd floor at end of hall, room #208, daily 6:30 P.M.; Mon., Sat. 9 A.M.; Sun. 11:30 A.M. Most meetings are nonsmoking. There's an 8 P.M. smoking meeting some nights. NA, Tues.,

Thurs., Sat. 5 P.M. OA, Tues. 8 P.M. ALANON, Mon. 5 P.M. CODA, Fri. 8 P.M. Call Angela, phone: (322) 2-3906.

San Blas, Nay.

Check at McDonald's restaurant for times. Mon., Wed., Fri. 6 P.M.; Sun. 9:30 A.M. Calle Sinaloa #19 (sort of). Little shopping center across from police station. All the way in back. Go through gate to back patio.

San Carlos, Son.

At Catholic Church by marina, Mon.–Fri. 7:30 P.M., Sat. 9:30 A.M. Thanks to B.C.

Yelapa, Jal.

Wed., Sat. 5:30 P.M. Ask at Mike's house on the beach.

Zihuatanejo/Ixtapa, Gro.

Go on the canal road toward Playa Madero. Pass la Boquita Bakery. Turn right toward Hotel Solimar. On one side of the plaza is the Spanish meeting. Across the plaza is the English-speaking group. Meet at 6 P.M. on Thurs.

Colonial Mexico

Chapala, Jal.—Ajijic Area

Little Chapel, Mon., 4 P.M.; Río Zula #1, Tues.; ACOA, Hidalgo #63, Ajijic; ALANON, Río Zula #1, Wed. 4 P.M.; Río Zula #1, Thur., 4 P.M.; ALANON, Río Zula #1, Sat., 9:30 A.M.

Cuernavaca, Mor.

Check the *Mexico City News* for times and locations.

Guadalajara, Jal.

Clubhouse, Filadelfia #2015 (off Lopez Mateos and Las Américas, near Brazz Restaurant), Mon., Wed. 7:30 P.M.

Mexico, D.F.

Río Danubio #39 (upstairs), Mon., Wed., Fri. 2 P.M.; Tues., Thurs. 8 P.M.; Sat. 4 P.M.; Sun. 6 P.M. Union Church, Reforma 1870, Mon., Wed., Fri.

8 P.M. Ladies meeting, Nuestra Señora de Guadalupe, Corner Prado Sur y Virreyes (Basement), Wed. 4 P.M. Phone: (5) 568-5104, 525-9090.

San Miguel Allende, Gto.

This group moves around a lot, but the most recent address is: Alano Club, Jesus 25A, upstairs, AA every night at 6:30 P.M. Also ALANON, Artists in Recovery, OA, CODA, NA. Check the paper *Atencion* for details.

Yucatán

Cancún, Q.R.

AA English-speaking meetings at the Cancún International Group, 6:15 P.M. every day downtown at the Plaza Centro shopping center, Av. Nader, 3rd floor. Also noon Mon., Wed., Fri. Call Victoria, phone: (98) 84-0969.

Cozumel, Q.R.

Tabla de Salvación, 632 20th Av. South, between 7th and 9th Sts., Sun., Mon., Wed., Fri. 6 P.M.

Playa del Carmen, Q.R.

AA (English), at the Playacar school, just down from the Continental Plaza Hotel, on Calle 10. See gate guard for exact location. Mon., Wed., Fri. 5 or 5:30 P.M.

U.S. Consulates and Consular Agents for All Mexico

These, too, are subject to change but were accurate at press time.

EMBASSY

American Embassy is located at Paseo de la Reforma 305, Col. Cuauhtémoc, 06500 **Mexico, D.F.** Phone: (52-5) 211-0042.

CONSULATES

Ciudad Juarez, Chih.

López Mateos #924-N CP, 32000. Phone: (16) 13-4048, 13-5050. Fax: (16) 16-9056. Duty Officer: (915) 526-6066 (in El Paso, Texas). Office hours:

08:00–15:45. Mailing address: American Consulate, APDO Postal #1681, 32000 Cd. Juarez, Chih.

Guadalajara, Jal.

Progreso #175 CP. Phone: (3) 625-2998. Fax: (3) 626-6549. Duty Officer and after-hours calls: (3) 626-5553. Office hours: 08:00–16:30. Mailing address: APDO Postal #39-10, 44171 Guadalajara, Jal.

Hermosillo, Son.

Monterrey #141 CP, 83260. Phone: (62) 17-2575. Fax: (62) 17-2578. Office hours: 08:00–16:45. Mailing address: American Consulate, APDO Postal #972, 83260 Hermosillo, Son.

Matamoros, Tamps.

Calle Primera #2002. Phone: (881) 2-4402. Fax: (881) 2-2171. Office hours: 08:00–12:00 and 13:00–17:00. Mailing address: American Consulate, APDO Postal #451, 87350 Matamoros, Tamps.

Mérida, Yuc.

Paseo Montejo #453. Phone: (99) 25-5011. Fax: (99) 25-6219. Office hours: 07:30–16:00. Mailing address: American Consulate, APDO Postal #130, 97000 Mérida, Yuc.

Monterrey, N.L.

Av. Constitución #411 Pte. CP, 64000 Monterrey, N.L. Phone: (83) 45-2120. Fax: (83) 45-7748. Mailing address: P.O. Box 3098, Laredo, TX 78044-3098.

Nuevo Laredo

Calle Allende #3330 Col. Jardín CP, 88260 Nuevo Laredo, Tamps. Phone: (871) 4-0696, 4-0512. Fax: (871) 4-0696, ext. 128. Duty Officer: (210) 763-1351 (cellular phone in Laredo, Texas). Office hours: 08:00–12:30 and 13:30–17:00. Mailing address: American Consulate, APDO Postal #38, 88260 Nuevo Laredo, Tamps.

Tijuana, B.C.N.

Tapachula #96. Phone: (66) 81-7400. Fax: (66) 81-8016. Duty Officer: (619)

585-2000 (paging service in San Diego, California). Office hours: 08:00–16:30. Mailing address: APDO Postal #68, 22420 Tijuana, B.C.

U.S. CONSULAR AGENTS

Acapulco, Gro.

Julie Mendez, Hotel Club del Sol, Costera Alemán Esq. Reyes Católicos, 19300 Acapulco, Gro. Phone: (748) 5-7207, 5-6600. Fax: (748) 5-7207.

Cabo San Lucas

Robin Hann, Blvd. Marian y Pedregal, Local 3, Zona Centro. Phone/Fax: (114) 3-3566.

Cancún, Q.R.

Lorraine H. Lara, Av. Nadar 40-Super Manzana 2A Edificio Marruecos, 3rd floor #31, 77500 Cancún, Q.R. Phone: (98) 84-2411, 84-6399. Fax: (98) 84-8222.

Mazatlán, Sin.

Gerianne Nelson, Hotel Playa Mazatlán, Rodolfo Loyaza #207 Zona Dorada, 82100 Mazatlán, Sin. Phone/Fax: (69) 16-5889 (ask for consular agent).

Oaxaca, Oax.

Mark Arnold Leyes, Alcala #201 Desp. 206, 68000 Oaxaca, Oax. Phone/Fax: (951) 4-3054.

Pto. Vallarta, Jal.

Parian del Puente, Local 12-A, 48300 Pto. Vallarta, Jal. Phone: (322) 2-0069. Fax: (322) 3-0074. Mailing address: APDO Postal #462, Pto. Vallarta, Jal.

San Luis Potosí, S.L.P.

Kathleen Reza, Francisco de P. Moriel #103-10, Col. Centro, 96000 San Luis Potosí, S.L.P. Phone/Fax: (481) 2-1528.

San Miguel de Allende, Gto.

Col. Philip J. Maher, Hernández Macías #72, CP, 37700 San Miguel de Allende, Gto. Phone: (465) 2-2357, 2-0068. Fax: (465) 2-1588. Mailing address: APDO Postal #328, San Miguel de Allende, Gto.

Tampico, Tam.

Elizabeth Alzaga, Ejército Mexicano #503-203, Col. Guadalupe, 89120 Tampico, Tam. Phone/Fax: (12) 13-2217.

Veracruz, Ver.

Edwin Culp, Víctimas del 25 de Junio #388, 91700 Veracruz, Ver. Phone: (29) 31-5821. Fax: (29) 31-6941.

Canadian Consulates and Embassies

Mexico City

The Canadian Chancery is at: Schiller 529, Col. Polanco, 11580 Mexico, D.F. Phone: 724-7900. Mailing address: APDO Postal #105-05, 11580 Mexico, D.F. Free call from anywhere in Mexico: 91-800-706-29. MITNET: 379-3000. Fax: (Administration) 724-7980, (Public affairs) 724-7981, (Trade) 724-7982, 724-7984, (Immigration) 724-7983, (HOM/Political) 724-7985. MITNET Fax: (Administration) 379-3900, (Public affairs) 379-3904, (Trade) 379-3902, (Immigration) 379-3901, (HOM/Political) 379-3914.

Acapulco, Gro.

The Consulate of Canada, Hotel Club del Sol, Costera Miguel Aleman Esq. Reyes Católicos, Acapulco, Gro. Mailing address: The Consulate of Canada, APDO Postal #94-C, 39300 Acapulco, Gro. Phone: (011-52-74) 85-6621. Fax: (011-52-74) 86-7417. Honorary Consul: Mrs. D. McLean. Territory includes the states of Guerrero and Michoacán.

Ajijic, Jal.

The Consulate of Canada, Hotel Real de Chapala, Paseo del Prado 20, Ajijic, Jal. Phone: (011-52-376) 62-420. Fax: (011-52-376) 62-420. Honorary Consul: Mr. A. C. Rose. Territory includes the municipalities of Chapala and Jocotepec, including Ajijic, San Antonio Tlyacapan and San Juan Cosala.

Cancún, Q.R.

The Consulate of Canada, Centro Comercial Plaza Mexico, Local 312, Av.

Tulum, 200 Esq. Agua, 77500 Cancún, Q.R. Phone: (011-52-98) 84-3716. Fax: (011-52-98) 62420. Honorary Consul: Mr. O. Lavole. Territory includes the states of Campeche Yucatan and Quintana Roo.

Guadalajara, Jal.

The Consulate of Canada, Hotel Fiesta Americana, Local 31, Aurelio Aceves 225, Col. Vallarta Pte., 44100 Guadalajara, Jal. Phone: (011-52-3) 616-5642, 615-6270, 615-62, 615-6266. Fax: (011-52-3) 615-8665. Consul and Trade Commissioner: Ms. J. Dauberry. Territory includes the state of Jalisco except Pto. Vallarta, Chapala Lake region and Jalisco Coast.

Mazatlán, Sin.

The Consulate of Canada, Hotel Playa Mazatlán, Zona Dorada, Rodolfo Loiza 202, 82110 Mazatlán, Sin.

Monterrey, N.L.

The Consulate of Canada, Edificio Kalos, Piso C-1, Local 108-A, Zaragoza 1300 Sur y Constitución, 6400 Monterrey, N.L. Phone: (011-52-8) 344-2753, 344-2906, 344-2961, 344-3200. Fax: (011-52-8) 344-3048. Vice Consul and Trade Commissioner: Mr. T. G. Cullen. Territory includes the states of Chihuahua, Coahuila, Nuevo Leon, San Luis Potosí, Tamaulipas and Zacatecas.

Oaxaca, Oax.

The Consulate of Canada, 119 Dr. Liceaga #8, 68000 Oaxaca, Oax. Mailing address: The Consulate of Canada, APDO Postal #29A Sucursal C, Col. Reforma, 68050 Oaxaca, Oax. Phone: (011-52-322) 33-777. Fax: (011-52-322) 52-147. Honorary Consul: Ms. F. May. Territory includes the states of Oaxaca and Chiapas.

Pto. Vallarta

The Consulate of Canada, Calle Hidalgo 226, 160 Zaragoza, Interior 10, Col. Centro, 46300 Pto. Vallarta, Jal. Phone: (011-52-322) 253-98. Fax: (011-52-322) 235-17. Honorary Consul: Ms. L. Benoit. Territory includes Pto. Vallarta, Jalisco Coast and the states of Colima and Nayarit.

San Miguel de Allende, Gto.

The Consulate of Canada, Mesones 38, Interior 15, 37700 San Miguel de Allende, Gto. Phone: (011-52-415) 230-25. Fax: (011-52-415) 268-56. Honorary Vice Consul: Ms. G. Bisaillion. Territory includes the states of Guanajuato and Querétaro.

Tijuana, B.C.

The Consulate of Canada, German Gedovius 10411-101, Condominio del Parque, Zona Rio, 22320 Tijuana, B.C.N. Phone: (011-52-66) 84-0461. Fax: (011-52-66) 84-0301. Honorary Consul: Mr. R. E. Ripa. Territory includes the states of Baja California Norte and Baja California Sur and Sonora.

American Legion Posts in Mexico

You can find plenty of friends at the many posts in Mexico. The phone numbers and addresses are not always home or post numbers.

Acapulco, Gro.

Post #4, Emilio Carranza: APDO Postal #1477, 39300 Acapulco, Gro. Phone: (74) 83-9357. Meets at Acapulco Yacht Club. Commander: Ken Honett; Adjutant: Dean Geddes. Phone: (74) 66-0462.

Post #7, Lake Chapala: APDO Postal #31, 4590 Chapala, Jal. Phone: (3) 765-2259. Commander: Mike Valentine; Adjutant: Bob Martin.

Cuernavaca, Mor.

Post #10: APDO Postal #4-464, 62460 Volcanos, Cuernavaca, Mor. Phone: (73) 15-6276, 17-2509. Commander: Fred Bach; Adjutant: Ken Smythe. APDO Postal #1-1623, 62000 Cuernavaca, Mor.

Guadalajara, Jal.

Post #3, Alvarez Castillo: San Antonio #143, APDO Postal #31-401, Col. Las Fuentes 4, Guadalajara, Jal. Phone: (3) 631-1208. Commander: Bill Gillohm; Adjutant: Royce Wheeler.

Mazatlán, Sin.

Post #11: APDO Postal #154-B, Centra Camionera 82, Mazatlán, Sin.

Phone: (69) 84-1003, 83-8787. Commander: Frank Montoya; Adjutant: Ray Robins.

Mexico, D.F.

Post #2, Alan Seeger: Celaya #25, Col. Hipodromo Condesa, 06100 Mexico, D.F. Phone: (5) 564-3386. Rest./Bar: (5) 574-4053. Fax: (5) 564-3386. Has Happy Hours. Commander: Ray F. Buggs; Adjutant: Robert F. Fox.

Post #18, Billy Payne: Chilpanzingo #46, Col. Roma Sur, 06760 Mexico, D.F. Phone: (5) 553-4383. Commander: Marv. Gottlieb; Adjutant: William P. McIntosh.

Monterrey, N.L.

Post #5, Steve Fordham: APDO Postal #280, Col. B. Del Valle, 66250 Garza Garcia, N.L. Phone: (83) 56-8293. Fax: (83) 42-5517. Commander: Ernesto DeKaratry; Adjutant: Raymond Orrell.

San Miguel de Allende, Gto.

Post #6, Thomas V. Price: APDO Postal #331, 37700 San Miguel de Allende, Gto. Phone: (415) 52-0764. Commander: John V. Fleming; Adjutant: Simon B. Gonzalez.

Post #8, Raymond Howard: APDO Postal #218, 37700 San Miguel de Allende, Gto. Phone: (415) 2-3115. Commander: Tom Proulx; Adjutant: Jack Hines.

Mexican Government Tourism Offices— United States and Canada

The Mexican Government Tourism Offices have changed dramatically in the past several months.

UNITED STATES

Chicago

300 N. Michigan Ave., 4th Fl., Chicago, IL 60601. Phone: 321-606-9252. Fax: 312-606-9012.

Houston
10440 Westoffice, Houston, TX 77042. Phone: 713-629-1611. Fax: 713-629-1837.

Los Angeles
2401 W. 6th St., 5th Fl., Los Angeles, CA 90057. Phone: 213-351-2069. Fax: 213-351-2074.

Miami
1200 NW 78th St., Ste. 203, Miami, FL 33126. Phone: 305-718-4091. Fax: 305-718-4098.

New York
21 E. 63rd St., 3rd Fl., New York, NY 10021. Phone: 212-821-0313. Fax: 212-821-0367.

Orlando
Avenue of the Stars, EPCOT Center, Lake Buena Vista, FL 32830. Phone: 407-827-5350.

Washington, D.C.
1911 Pennsylvania Ave. NW, Washington, D.C. 20006. Phone: 202-728-1750. Fax: 202-728-1758.

CANADA

Montreal
One Place Ville Marie, Ste. 1931, Montreal, Quebec H3B 2C3, Canada. Phone: 514-871-1052. Fax: 514-871-3825.

Toronto
2 Floor St. West, Ste. 1801, Toronto, Ontario M4W 3E2, Canada. Phone: 416-925-0704. Fax: 416-925-6061.

Vancouver
999 W. Hastings, Ste. 1110, Vancouver, B.C. V6C 2W2, Canada. Phone: 604-669-2845. Fax: 604-669-3498.

For general information and brochures about Mexico, call 1-800-44-MEXICO. For all Mexico, call 91-800-90-3-92; Nuevo Leon: 91-800-8-32-22; Sonora: 91-800-6-25-55.

Mexico's Spanish-Language Schools

The following list was graciously provided by Ron Mader, whose website, Eco Travels in Latin America (www.planeta.com), is one of the neatest around. Please support him in his work and visit his site for more information. E-mail: ron@greenbuilder.com.

1999 Directory of Spanish Language Schools (Version 3.3, Feb. 1997), compiled by Ron Mader, www.2planeta.com/mader/ecotravel/schools/school1st.htm.htm#mx. The Directory of Spanish Language Schools began its third year online in 1997. This a regularly updated index of the schools where you can learn or improve your Spanish in a Latin American country. This inclusive directory is posted online in the Eco Travels in Latin America website (www.planeta.com) and e-mailed free of charge to anyone who requests it. The list may be freely copied and reproduced if the source is given. If you operate a school, you can also submit a listing.

Cultural and linguistic immersion has numerous benefits. Plus, the food is generally better than a college cafeteria. When you send an inquiry to a school, let the director know about this directory. If you're a regular visitor to the Eco Travels website, your support means a great deal!

OAXACA

"Sol y Tierra" Spanish Language Institute, Xicotencatl No. 212, Oaxaca, Oax. Contact: Rogelio Ballesteros. Phone: New line being installed, please fax or e-mail. Fax: (951) 5-21-25. E-mail: soltierr@antequera.com. Web: www.mexonline.com/soltierr.htm.

Instituto de Comunicación y Cultura, M. Alcalá #307-12, Col. Centro, 68000 Oaxaca, Oax. Contacts: Yolanda Garcia Caballero and Warren Lyle. Phone/Fax: (951) 634-43. E-mail: info@iccoax.com. Web: www.iccoax.com.

Centro de Idiomas, Universidad Autónoma Benito Juarez de Oaxaca, APDO Postal #523, 68000 Oaxaca, Oax. Phone/Fax: (951) 65922.

Instituto Cultural Oaxaca, APDO Postal #340, 68000 Oaxaca, Oax. Phone: (951) 5-34-04. Fax: (951) 5-37-28.

Becari Escuela de Español y Ingles, M. Bravo 210, 68000 Oaxaca, Oax.

Phone/Fax: (951) 46076.

SAN CRISTOBAL DE LAS CASAS

Universidad Autonoma de Chiapas, Av. Hidalgo 1, Dpto de Lenguas, San Cristobal de las Casas, Chiapas.

Instituto Jovel, Maria Adelina Flores 21, APDO Postal #62, San Cristobal de las Casas, Chiapas. Phone/Fax: (967) 84069.

Centro Bilingue, Calle Real de Guadalupe 55, San Cristobal de las Casas, Chiapas. Contact: Roberto Rivas, Director. Phone/Fax: (967) 83723. U.S. Phone: 1-800-303-4983.

CUERNAVACA

Cemanahuac Educational Community, Col. Las Palmas, San Juan #4, Cuernavaca, Mor. Mailing address: APDO Postal #5-21, Cuernavaca, Mor. Contact: Vivian B. Harvey. Phone: (73) 18-6407, 14-2988. Fax: (73) 12-5418. E-mail: 74052.2570@compuserve.com. For a brochure, call Ann O'Neill in the United States at 1-800-247-6651.

Experiencia–Centro de Intercambio Bilingue y Cultural, APDO Postal #C-96, Cuernavaca, Mor. Contact: Sherry Howell Williams. Phone: (73) 12-65-79. Fax: (73) 18-52-09. U.S. Phone: (512) 331-5925. U.S. Fax: (512) 257-7237. E-mail: experiencia@weblane.com. Web: www.weblane.com/experiencia/.

Encuentros Comunicación y Cultura, APDO Postal #2-71, Calle Morelos 36, Col. Acapantzingo, 62440 Cuernavaca, Mor. Phone: (73) 12-50-88. E-mail: encuent@infosel.net.mxorencuent@microweb.com.mx. Web: www.cuernavaca.infosel.com.mx/encuentros/spanish.htm.

Escuela Azteca, Río Usumacinta 710, Col. Vista Hermosa. Phone: (73) 1524-69. Cuauhnahuac, APDO Postal #5-26, 62051 Cuernavaca, Mor. Phone: (73) 12-36-73.

Cuernavaca Spanish Institute, Av. Plan de Ayala 513-B, Col. Los Volcanes, Cuernavaca, Mor. Phone: (73) 16-25-83. Fax: (73) 15-60-19.

Ideal Latinoamérica, APDO Postal #2-65, Priv. Narciso Mendoza 107, Col. Pradera, 62158 Cuernavaca, Mor. Phone: (73) 11-7551. Fax: (73) 11-5910.

Centro de Artes y Lenguas (CALE), P.O. Box 1777, 06200 Cuernavaca, Mor. Contact: Xavier Sotel. Phone: (73) 13-06-03, 17-31-26. Fax: (73) 13-73-52.

The Mexican Immersion Center, P.O. Box 4-193, 62431 Cuernavaca, Mor. Contact: Dalel Cortes. Phone: (73) 22-10-83. Fax: (73) 15-79-53.

Mérida

Instituto de Español Moderno, Av. 21 No. 195 x 12, Col. Mexico Oriente, Mérida, Yuc. Phone: (99) 25-95-28. Fax: (99) 26-94-17.

Centro de Idiomas Sureste (CIS), Calle 66 No. 535 x 57, Edificio Alejandra, Upstairs, Mérida, Yuc. Contact: Chloe Pacheco. Phone: (99) 23-09-54. Fax: (99) 23-37-36.

Veracruz

La Florida Rainforest Center, Rancho La Florida, Peruela, Veracruz. Phone: (271) 66501. U.S. address: Social Science Department, Central Oregon Community College, 2600 NW College Way, Bend, OR 97701. Phone: (541) 383-7237. Fax: (541) 383-7503. Note: School operates only in the summer.

Mexico City

Hablasa, Amsterdam 76-2, Col. Hipodromo Condesa, Mexico, D.F. Phone: 553-2509.

Pto. Vallarta

Centro International, Libertad y Miramar No. 47 #1, Pto. Vallarta. Phone: 3-2082. Fax: 3-2982.

Morelia

Centro Mexicano Internacional (CMI), Calz. Fray. Antonio de San Miguel 173, Morelia, Mich. Phone: (32) 12-4596.

Baden-Powell Institute, Antonio Alzate 565, Morelia, Mich. Phone: (32) 24070.

Guadalajara

Centro de Estudios para Extranjeros, Universidad de Guadalajara, APDO Postal #1-2130, 44100 Guadalajara, Jal. Phone: (3) 653-60-24.

Guanajuato

Instituto Falcón, Callejón de la Mora 158, 36000 Guanajuato, Gto. Con-

tact: Jorge Barroso. Fax: (473) 2-36-94. E-mail: falcon@bajio.infonet.
com.mx. Web: www.infonet.com.mx/falcon.

San Miguel de Allende

Academia Hispano Americana, Mesones 4, 37700 San Miguel de Allende,
Gto. Phone: (415) 2-03-49. Fax: (415) 2-23-33.

Instituto "Habla Hispana," Calzada de la Luz #25, 37700 San Miguel de
Allende, Gto. Contact: Angelica Rodriguez, Director. Phone/Fax: (415)
2-07-13.

Colima

Language Institute of Colima. Phone: 2-05-87, 4-57-86. U.S. address: P.O.
Box 827, Miranda, CA 95553. Phone: 1-800-604-6547.

Ensenada

Center of Languages. U.S. Contact: 5066 La Jolla Blvd., Ste. 116, La Jolla,
CA 92037. Phone: 1-800-834-2256, 619-454-7900. Fax: 619-688-
1853.

Bibliography

Newsletters About Mexico

There are some fine newsletters printed by very dedicated people. All are different and reflect the personal opinions of the authors. Most will provide you with a sample for a minimal fee, say $6 to cover postage and their trouble. If you are thinking of living in Mexico, these can be great assets.

AIM (Adventures in Mexico) is a good source of everyday living costs in Mexico. It features interviews with Americans and Canadians who have retired there. They also do a feature story every issue about some less well-known locales. Quite a good reference. Bimonthly. APDO Postal #31-70, 45050 Guadalajara, Jal., Mexico. $16 yearly.

Latin America Travel & Business Report is a slick, two-color job that covers all of Latin America, from Mexico, Central America, Cuba to South America. It is eclectic, with stories on news, retiring, working, doing business, fishing, spas and general travel. It has featured articles on starting a business, finding an apartment, doing business, driving in Mexico, RVing in South America, how to take your pet to Mexico, how to live in Guatemala and fishing in Mexico, Belize and South America. Eclectic, huh? A rock-and-roll musician, Joe "King" Carrasco, irregularly (what else would you expect) contributes articles, including a series called "The Mexican Jukebox." Quarterly. 1116 Ave. L, Galveston, TX 77550-6135. Sample $6. $29.95 yearly. Online $15.95; CD-ROM $18.95. Order from 1-800-321-5605 or at www.mexicomike.com.

Mexican Meanderings is published by a couple in Austin, Texas, the Felsteads. They travel by car all over the country. When they get back, they inform the rest of us what it was like. They will tell you about out-of-the-way places as well as those on the beaten track. They give great reviews to little-known books. Southwind Information Services, P.O. Box 33057, Austin, TX 78764. $18 yearly, six issues. E-mail: mexplore@vakise.com.

Mexico Living & Travel Update is written by John and Jean Bryant, who actually live in Guadalajara. There is no better source for up-to-the-minute prices and the straight skinny on what it's really like to live in Mexico. Quarterly. MRTA, P.O. Box 2190, Ste. 23, Pahrump, NV 89041-2190. $25 yearly. Single copy, $8.

People's Guide Travel Letter is written by Carl Franz and Lorena Havens, authors of *The People's Guide to Mexico,* a classic read. The newsletter is lively and informative. It is published irregularly. It is good for anyone, but has articles for the young in spirit who want to backpack and see the "real" Mexico. 15100 SE 38th St., Ste. 806, Bellevue, WA 98006. $15 for four issues, $5 for a single issue. They will credit you for the $5 if you subscribe.

Travel Mexico is published by the *Travellers Guide to Mexico* people. It has information on the tourist industry and interesting tidbits of newsy information on present-day Mexico. Bimonthly. APDO Postal #6-1007, 06600 Mexico, D.F., Mexico. $15 yearly.

Books

Breaking Out of Beginning Spanish by Joseph J. Keenan is the best Spanish-language book I have ever seen. It is not for rank beginners, but is dandy for those who have some grounding in the language. It will help you to avoid some of the common errors that brand you as a gringo who learned your language in school. Published by the University of Texas Press, P.O. Box 7819, Austin, TX 78713-7819. Available at bookstores. $14.95.

Drive Mexico—How, Where, Why by "Mexico" Mike Nelson. ISBN 1-889489-07-7. The only book that tells you how to drive and where and where not to drive in Mexico. Based on twenty years of driving a million miles, this book could save your trip and help you decide if driving is for you. Don't be misled by those who have not done it. Driving can be the best and safest way to know Mexico. $12.95 plus $3 S&H, from Roads Scholar Press, 1116 Ave. L, Galveston, TX 77550-6135. Phone: 1-800-321-5605.

The Gringo's Investment Guide by Ginger Combs–Ramirez is straightforward and easy to read. It concentrates on the ins and outs of buying real estate in Mexico. It is based on personal experience as well as on interviews with experts. Before buying property, be sure to buy this book. Monmex Publishing, P.O. Box 1158, Ennis, MT 59729. Phone: 1-800-883-2712. $24.95.

How to Buy Real Estate in Mexico by Dennis John Peyton is the definitive resource on buying property in Mexico. Dennis is a lawyer licensed to practice both in Mexico and in the United States. Consequently, the advice he gives is accurate, if somewhat lawyerly. If you really want to know what you are doing, get this book. Although there are some differences of opinion between *The Gringo's Investment Guide* (see above) and Peyton's book, you should read them both before signing on the dotted line. Law-Mexico Publishing, 2220 Otay Lakes Road, Ste. 502, East Lake, CA 91915. Phone: 1-800-LAW-MEXICO. $24.95.

Mexico from the Driver's Seat is a collection of travel essays and straightforward reporting will give you an insight into the character of the Mexican people and whet your appetite for Mexico, from the well-known attractions to those off-the-beaten track. The stories are funny, spiritual and entertaining, and some are downright outlandish. Warning—it has encouraged more people to take off to Mexico than you can count. $8.95.

Mexico Living and Travel by John Bryant, who lives in Mexico. My little book *(Live Better South of the Border in Mexico)* gives you a taste of what it is like to live there. His book is the full-course dinner. It is geared more to the retiree than the businessman or the bohemian. $29.95 with S&H from: MRTA, P.O. Box 2190, Ste. 23, Pahrump, NV 89041-2190.

Mexico's Colonial Heart is a complete driver's guide to the heartland of Mexico. You can travel by vehicle with Mike as your personal tour guide. For those who want to fly into Mexico City and rent a car, he even includes detailed directions for getting out of the Mexico City airport from the rental car pickup area. It covers a rough rectangle with Mexico City and Guadalajara as its easternmost and westernmost points, San Miguel de Allende to the northeast and the spa Ixtapan de la Sal to the southwest. $19.95.

More Than a Dozen of Mexico's Hidden Jewels is a collecion of stories for the armchair adventurer about places that are truly unique. Journey to Xilitla, where an eccentric Englishman who was a friend of Dali, Picasso and Bogart built a surrealistic sculpture garden in an orchid jungle. Visit the Zone of Silence, where UFOs are reputed to land. Relax at El Paraiso, an ecological resort near the Texas border with unspoiled beaches where the endangered Kemp's Ridley sea turtles lay their eggs and flocks of parrots commute over your *cabaña*. Discover the little-known but exotic Gulf Coast and its Emerald Coast. Find an old-growth forest an hour from Mexico City. Many have used this book as a planning guide for their trips. $9.95

The People's Guide to Mexico by Carl Franz and Lorena Havens. Now in its twenty-fifth year, this is a classic. No travel guide, it is a cultural guide. This is the one book that tells you what living in Mexico is like from the ground up. It is aimed at those who want to understand the culture of Mexico and the Mexican people. Although much of the information is geared to those on a tight budget or those who live a bohemian lifestyle, it contains invaluable information applicable to everyone. Published by Muir Publications. Available at bookstores.

Spas & Hot Springs of Mexico, Second Edition by "Mexico" Mike Nelson. If you love to explore hot springs, if you love to be pampered in first-class spas or if holistic retreats are your desire, this is the book for you. No other book satisfies these diverse audiences. This unique book offers in-depth reviews, with Mike's personal picks and pans, covering more than thirty restful places from world-class spas to simple hot springs. The stories are funny, bittersweet and entertaining. The facts are accurate. When it comes to hot springs, there is nothing else to compare it to. *Mexico File* said *Spas & Hot Springs of Mexico* is "the Michelin and Zagat of the upscale, spiritual." *New Orleans Times-Picayune* said, "Nelson gives a synopsis of the spirit of the place." $16.95 plus $4 S&H, 1116 Ave. L, Galveston, TX 77550-6135. Phone: 1-800-321-5605. Available at bookstores.

Travellers Guide to Mexico, published in Mexico, is the best source for tourist and business information about Mexico City and the country. It is chock-full of color photographs and interesting articles. You will find it in all the top-notch hotels and at bookstores. Buy a copy if you want to know more about the culture, doing business in Mexico or if you intend to do any upscale traveling to the main tourist spots. Published by Prometur S.A. de C.V., Gral. Juan Cano 68, San Miguel Chapultepec, 11850 Mexico, D.F.

Guidebooks for Mexico I recommend are: *Lonely Planet* and *Moon Handbook.*

Internet and Mexico Websites

There are hundreds of websites about Mexico, with more born every day. Just go to Yahoo! or any other search engine and type "Mexico." You'll be amazed at the number of sites you find. You can also go to the news groups on America Online, CompuServe and Prodigy, though these tend to be more requests for information about places to go for tourist visits. You might even run into me.

I checked all the sites and deleted some. There are ISPs and Internet providers almost everywhere in Mexico now.

www.mexicomike.com is "Mexico" Mike's home page. Who knows what you'll find here? Driving tips, an interactive map, spas, stories about stuffed grandmothers, the Zone of Silence, where UFOs are supposed to land and spas. Mike's trips are added periodically. It should be funny and should have information on out-of-the-way places. It may be the best argument for limiting access to the web. "Mexico" Mike's e-mail address is mexicomike @mexicomike.com

www.spagetaway.com is a fascinating site about the spas of Mexico. Detailed descriptions and gorgeous photographs make this far more than a mere catalog of spas. Also includes spas in Costa Rica and the Dominican Republic. Reservations can be made online.

www.spa-mexico.com is yet another site about the spas of Mexico. It, too, is full of descriptions and pictures that make you want to go.

www.reforma.infosel.com has the *Reforma* newspaper in Spanish, which is one of the most respected papers in Mexico.

www.cityview.com covers all the bases for residents, tourists and business travelers. Apart from the usual information—hotels, restaurants, places to see, etc.—it is updated daily with information on museum exhibits, concerts and other current events. It is the most complete of the websites on Mexico City. It has sections for many U.S. cities too.

www.mexconnect.com is a fantastic source for retirement, living and travel information. This is a lively place with tons of information about living specifically in Guadalajara, Chapala and Ajijic as well as other places in Mexico. It is graphically rich and the content is varied. I like it.

www.teach-english-mexico.com is your one-stop shop for information on resources on teaching English in Mexico.

www.wotw.com/mexico has lots of information on travel, tourism, archeological sites, maps and more.

www.lonelyplanet.com has good stuff about the whole world, including Mexico. They produce fine guidebooks.

www.worldwide.edu/ci/mexico has a comprehensive list of language schools in Mexico with many U.S. contacts.

www.mexico-forwarding.com is the website of a company that specializes in forwarding household goods to and from Mexico.

www.mexico-realestate.com/mre is the organ of Mexico Real Estate & Travel. It has a variety of useful information about those subjects.

www.planeta.com is a fascinating source of ecologically oriented information about Mexico and Latin America. It also has an updated listing of language schools for all of Latin America. It has articles about little-known places and the sagas of the need for environmental concern versus the locals' needs for income. Voted one of the best web pages by several sources.

www.quick.com/mexico/ingles/ing.htm is provided by the Mexican government.

www.netcom.com/~rbeech/mex.html is a web page about Pto. Vallarta run by Randy Beech.

www.mexicoweb.com has information on Cancún and the area.

www.mexicoweb.com/travel/index.html is incredible. It has information on just about anything you could want in Mexico. Visit it.

www.tonyperez.com has an extensive library of well-known and little-known places and RV parks. The listings are based on Tony's visits.

www.goguatemala.com. If Guatemala is in your plans, you must visit this site!

www.hcampers.com is about camping and RVing in the southwestern United States and northern Mexico. Although some of the listings are optimistic, they are working on updating them.

www.adventuretrek.com. This RV caravan company specializes in Central America and South America. Some great RV links.

www.novedades.com.mx/the-news.htm is the site of the English-language newspaper *The News.* Good general information.

Several of Mexico's states have their own sites. You can access them through the Mexican government's tourism site: **www.quick.com/mexico/ingles/ing.htm.**

Index

About the Author

"MEXICO" MIKE NELSON has lived and traveled in Mexico for thirty years, both as someone counting his pennies and as one who can afford the finer things in life. His knowledge of the country has been recognized by news media such as *The New York Times, The Wall Street Journal, The Washington Post, Los Angeles Times, The Dallas Morning News, Asian Wall Street Journal, Manchester* (England) *Guardian, London* (England) *Observer, Irish Times,* the Mexican Tourism Department and many more. He is frequently called upon by Hollywood to serve as a location scout for various films and TV shows.

A prolific author, tireless promoter, international lecturer and veteran of more than a hundred TV, radio and print interviews, "Mexico" Mike has formed a large and dedicated fan base through his popular website (www.mexicomike.com) and newsletter (to subscribe contact him by e-mail at mexicomike@mexicomike.com). He has published a dozen books on Mexico, as well as several magazine articles.

For three years he taught classes on international living and business at the Learning Annexes in Los Angeles, San Francisco and San Diego. He currently teaches those classes, as well as classes on prosperity consciousness, in Galveston and Houston, Texas. He splits his time between homes in Galveston, Texas, and Cabo, Mexico.